A MODERN ATLAS OF AFRICAN HISTORY

A MODERN ATLAS
OF
AFRICAN HISTORY

G. S. P. FREEMAN-GRENVILLE

Cartography E. HAUSMAN

REX COLLINGS LONDON 1976

First published by Rex Collings Ltd.
69 Marylebone High Street, London W1
& produced by Carta Ltd.

This book is available both as a Hardback
and as a Paperback edition.

ISBN 0860 36 0091 (Paperback)
ISBN 0860 36 0113 (Hardback)

Preface

This atlas originated from requests for a school atlas of African history from African headmasters and history teachers, and was prepared in paperback form together with a preface and instructions suitable for school use. It covers the whole period from the earliest relics of prehistoric man in Africa up to 1975, a range substantially greater than any preceding atlas.

In responding to a fresh request for an edition for library use, it is necessary to explain the deliberate limitations of the work. Apart from prehistory, recorded history in Africa begins in Egypt c.3100 B.C. Since then there have been great numbers of African empires, states and acephalous societies that have preceded the some fifty independent states of today. To account for the fortunes and vicissitudes of them all in an area which is more than twice as large as Europe, and more than 800 can be identified, would require a very large atlas indeed. The seventy maps of this atlas are designed solely to illustrate the more important themes, facts, episodes or sequences of events, which have been detailed in a skeletal form in my *Chronology of African History,* 1973, and can be used in conjunction with it.

The Select Bibliography lists the more important works consulted. A complete bibliography of all the historical and geographical works employed, including texts in Greek, Latin, Arabic, Swahili, French, Italian and Portuguese, together with the reference books, atlases, journals and newspapers that have also been used, would take up so much space as to make the work unwieldy. It has been thought more important to provide an exhaustive gazetteer. In this the number of each map is given first, the letters A,B,C, and so on, providing longitudinal references, and 1,2,3, and so on, showing latitudinal references.

There are very many who have given me their advice and assistance, so many that it would be tedious to mention them all. They, especially my African friends, have my deepest gratitude.

Sheriff Hutton,
York,
25 November 1975.

G.S.P.F.-G.

List of Maps

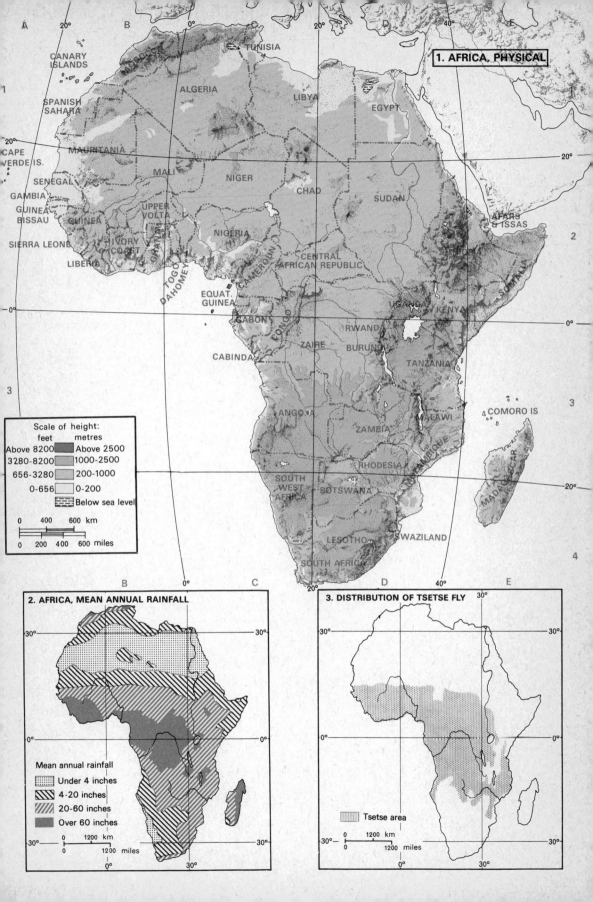

1. AFRICA, PHYSICAL

CANARY
ISLANDS

SPANISH
SAHARA

MOROCCO

TUNISIA

ALGERIA

LIBYA

EGYPT

CAPE
VERDE IS.

MAURITANIA

MALI

NIGER

CHAD

SUDAN

AFARS
& ISSAS

SENEGAL

GAMBIA

GUINEA
BISSAU

GUINEA

UPPER
VOLTA

NIGERIA

CENTRAL
AFRICAN REPUBLIC

SIERRA LEONE

IVORY
COAST

CAMEROUN

SOMALIA

LIBERIA

TOGO
DAHOMEY

EQUAT.
GUINEA

GABON

CONGO

ZAIRE

UGANDA

KENYA

RWANDA

BURUNDI

TANZANIA

CABINDA

ANGOLA

ZAMBIA

MALAWI

COMORO IS

MADAGASCAR

RHODESIA

MOZAMBIQUE

SOUTH
WEST
AFRICA

BOTSWANA

SWAZILAND

LESOTHO

SOUTH AFRICA

Scale of height:
feet	metres
Above 8200	Above 2500
3280-8200	1000-2500
656-3280	200-1000
0-656	0-200

Below sea level

0   400   600 km

0   200   400   600 miles

2. AFRICA, MEAN ANNUAL RAINFALL

Mean annual rainfall

Under 4 inches

4-20 inches

20-60 inches

Over 60 inches

0   1200 km

0   1200 miles

3. DISTRIBUTION OF TSETSE FLY

Tsetse area

0   1200 km

0   1200 miles

4. THE EARLY STONE AGE

Rabat
Temara △ Ternifin △ Sidi Zin
Sidi Abdurrahman ▲ Casablanca Ain Hanech

Tachengit △

Tihodaine △

Libyan Desert
Kharga △

Senegal R.

Niger R.

Yayo ▲

Ethiopian Plateau
R. Awash
Sheik △
(2,500,000 BC)

Equator

Zaire R.

Kanyatsi ▲
(2,000,000 B.C.) Rusinga Is. △ Kanjera
Nsongezi △ Kanam
Zaire Basin Fort Ternan ▲ Olorgesailie
Laetolil ▲ △ Olduvai Gorge (c.490,000 B.C.)
Olduvai (c.1,800,000 B.C.)

Isimila
Kalambo Falls ▲
(c.55,300 B.C.)

Broken Hill
Zambezi R.
Ruvuma R.

Cunene R.

Victoria Falls △
Lochard
Kalahari Desert Cave of Hearths
Sterkfontein Makapan ▲
Kliplaatdrif Sterkfontein Extension
Taungs Swartkrans
Orange R. △ Kimberley

Hopefield △
Stellenbosch

---

5. HANDAXE CULTURES IN AFRICA, ASIA AND EUROPE

Distribution of handaxe culture

0   1200 km
0   1200 miles

▲ Sites related to Olduvai c.1,800,000 B.C.
△ Main sites after c.500,000 B.C.
• Other sites

0   500   1000   1500 km.
0   500   1000 miles

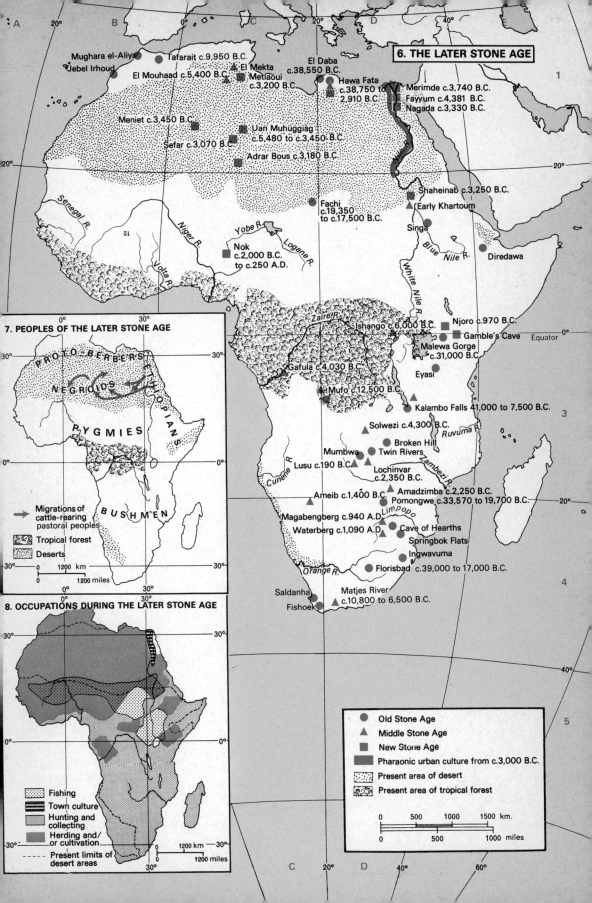

6. THE LATER STONE AGE

Mughara el-Aliya
Jebel Irhoud
El Mouhaad c.5,400 B.C.
Tafarait c.9,950 B.C.
El Mekta
Metlaoui c.3,200 B.C.
El Daba c.38,550 B.C.
Hawa Fata c.38,750 to 2,910 B.C.
Merimde c.3,740 B.C.
Fayyum c.4,381 B.C.
Nagada c.3,330 B.C.

Meniet c.3,450 B.C.
Uan Muhuggiag c.5,480 to c.3,450 B.C.
Sefar c.3,070 B.C.
Adrar Bous c.3,180 B.C.

Senegal R.
Niger R.
Volta R.
Yobe R.
Logane R.

Fachi c.19,350 to c.17,500 B.C.
Shaheinab c.3,250 B.C.
Early Khartoum
Singa
Diredawa

Nok c.2,000 B.C. to c.250 A.D.

Blue Nile R.
White Nile R.
Zaire R.

Ishango c.6,000 B.C.
Njoro c.970 B.C.
Gamble's Cave
Equator
Malewa Gorge c.31,000 B.C.
Gafula c.4,030 B.C.
Eyasi
Mufo c.12,500 B.C.
Kalambo Falls 41,000 to 7,500 B.C.

Ruvuma R.
Solwezi c.4,300 B.C.
Broken Hill
Mumbwa
Twin Rivers
Lusu c.190 B.C.
Lochinvar c.2,350 B.C.
Zambezi R.
Ameib c.1,400 B.C.
Amadzimba c.2,250 B.C.
Pomongwe c.33,570 to 19,700 B.C.
Cunene R.
Magabengberg c.940 A.D.
Limpopo
Waterberg c.1,090 A.D.
Cave of Hearths
Springbok Flats
Ingwavuma
Florisbad c.39,000 to 17,000 B.C.
Orange R.
Saldanha
Matjes River c.10,800 to 6,500 B.C.
Fishoek

7. PEOPLES OF THE LATER STONE AGE

PROTO-BERBERS
NEGROIDS
ETHIOPIANS
PYGMIES
BUSHMEN

→ Migrations of cattle-rearing pastoral peoples
Tropical forest
Deserts

0   1200 km
0   1200 miles

8. OCCUPATIONS DURING THE LATER STONE AGE

Fishing
Town culture
Hunting and collecting
Herding and/ or cultivation
--- Present limits of desert areas

1200 km
1200 miles

● Old Stone Age
▲ Middle Stone Age
■ New Stone Age
Pharaonic urban culture from c.3,000 B.C.
Present area of desert
Present area of tropical forest

0   500   1000   1500 km.
0   500   1000 miles

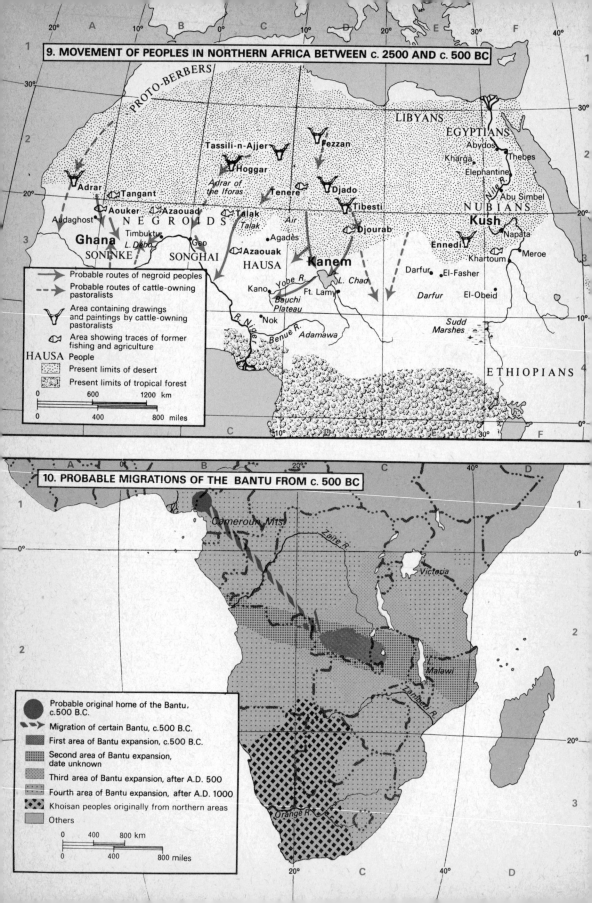

9. MOVEMENT OF PEOPLES IN NORTHERN AFRICA BETWEEN c. 2500 AND c. 500 BC

PROTO-BERBERS

LIBYANS

EGYPTIANS

Abydos
Kharga
Thebes
Elephantine

Tassili-n-Ajjer
Fezzan
Hoggar
Adrar of
the Iforas
Tenere
Djado
Adrar
Tangant
Tibesti
Abu Simbel

Aouker
Azaouad
Talak
NUBIANS

Audaghost
N E G R O I D S
Talak
Air
Djourab
KUSH
Napata

Ghana
Timbuktu
L. Débo
Gao
Agadès
Ennedi
Khartoum
Meroe

SONINKE
SONGHAI
Azaouak
Darfur
El-Fasher

HAUSA
Kanem
Darfur
El-Obeid

Kano
Yobe R.
Ft. Lamy
L. Chad

Bauchi
Plateau

R. Niger
Nok
Benue R.
Adamawa

Sudd
Marshes

ETHIOPIANS

	Probable routes of negroid peoples
	Probable routes of cattle-owning pastoralists
	Area containing drawings and paintings by cattle-owning pastoralists
	Area showing traces of former fishing and agriculture
HAUSA	People
	Present limits of desert
	Present limits of tropical forest

0   600   1200 km
0   400   800 miles

10. PROBABLE MIGRATIONS OF THE BANTU FROM c. 500 BC

Cameroun Mts.
Zaïre R.
Victoria
L. Malawi
Zambezi R.
Orange R.

	Probable original home of the Bantu, c.500 B.C.
	Migration of certain Bantu, c.500 B.C.
	First area of Bantu expansion, c.500 B.C.
	Second area of Bantu expansion, date unknown
	Third area of Bantu expansion, after A.D. 500
	Fourth area of Bantu expansion, after A.D. 1000
	Khoisan peoples originally from northern areas
	Others

0   400   800 km
0   400   800 miles

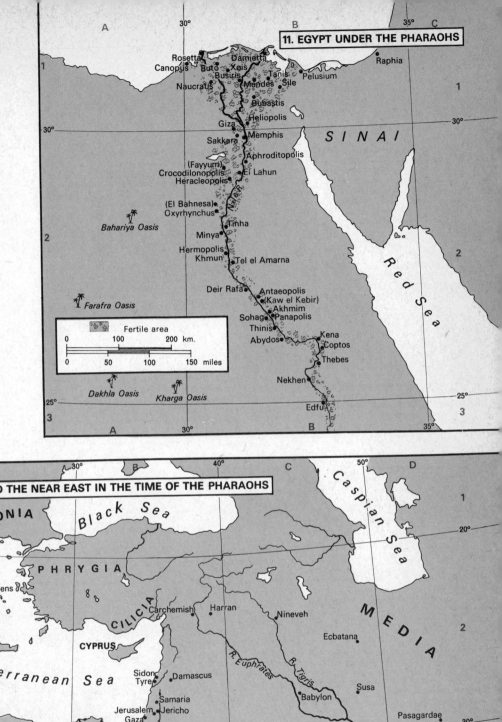

11. EGYPT UNDER THE PHARAOHS

Rosetta
Canopus
Buto
Busiris
Naucratis
Damietta
Xois
Mendes
Tanis
Sile
Pelusium
Raphia

Bubastis
Heliopolis
Giza
Memphis
Sakkara

S I N A I

Aphroditopolis
(Fayyum)
Crocodilonopolis
Heracleopolis
El Lahun

(El Bahnesa)
Oxyrhynchus
Tinha
Minya

Bahariya Oasis

Hermopolis
Khmun
Tel el Amarna

Deir Rafa
Antaeopolis
(Kaw el Kebir)
Akhmim
Panapolis
Sohag
Thinis
Abydos
Kena
Coptos
Thebes

Farafra Oasis

Red Sea

Nekhen

Edfu

Fertile area

| 0 | 100 | 200 km. |
| 0 | 50 | 100 | 150 miles |

Dakhla Oasis
Kharga Oasis

Nile

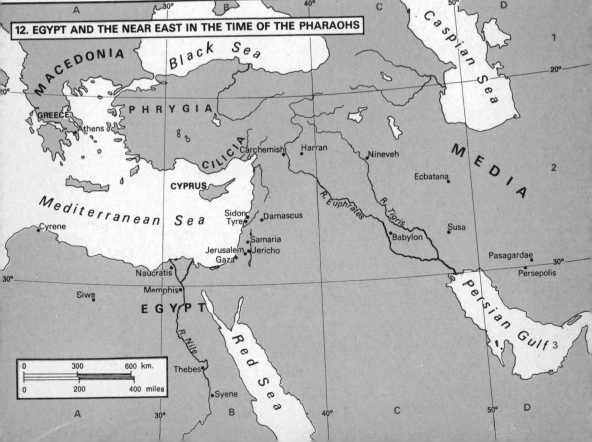

12. EGYPT AND THE NEAR EAST IN THE TIME OF THE PHARAOHS

MACEDONIA
Black Sea
Caspian Sea

GREECE
PHRYGIA
Athens
CILICIA
Carchemish
Harran
Nineveh
Ecbatana

M E D I A

CYPRUS

Mediterranean Sea

Sidon
Tyre
Damascus
R. Euphrates
R. Tigris
Babylon
Susa
Pasagardae
Persepolis

Cyrene

Samaria
Jerusalem
Jericho
Gaza

Naucratis

Siwa
Memphis

E G Y P T

Persian Gulf

R. Nile

Red Sea

Thebes

Syene

| 0 | 300 | 600 km. |
| 0 | 200 | 400 miles |

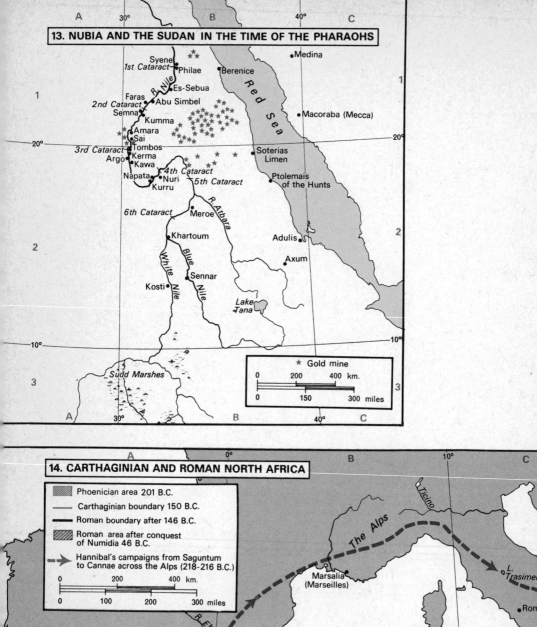

13. NUBIA AND THE SUDAN IN THE TIME OF THE PHARAOHS

• Medina

Syene
1st Cataract • Philae
Faras • Berenice
Es-Sebua
2nd Cataract • Abu Simbel
Semna • Kumma
Amara • Macoraba (Mecca)
Sai
Tombos
3rd Cataract • Kerma
Argo • Kawa
Napata • 4th Cataract
Nuri • 5th Cataract
Kurru

Soterias
Limen

Ptolemais
of the Hunts

6th Cataract • Meroe

Khartoum

Adulis

Axum

Sennar

Kosti

Lake
Tana

Sudd Marshes

R. Nile
Red Sea
R. Atbara
White Nile
Blue Nile

★ Gold mine

0	200	400 km.
0	150	300 miles

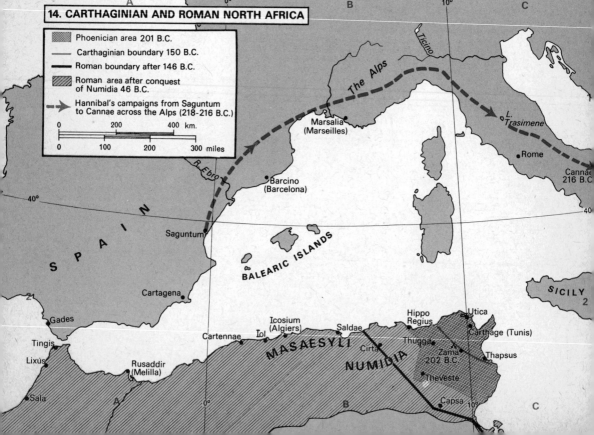

14. CARTHAGINIAN AND ROMAN NORTH AFRICA

▨	Phoenician area 201 B.C.
—	Carthaginian boundary 150 B.C.
▬	Roman boundary after 146 B.C.
▨	Roman area after conquest of Numidia 46 B.C.
➔	Hannibal's campaigns from Saguntum to Cannae across the Alps (218-216 B.C.)

0	200	400 km.
0	100	200	300 miles

The Alps

R. Ticino

Marsalia
(Marseilles)

L. Trasimene

Rome

Cannae
216 B.C.

R. Ebro

Barcino
(Barcelona)

Saguntum

BALEARIC ISLANDS

SPAIN

Cartagena

SICILY

Gades

Icosium
(Algiers)

Hippo
Regius

Utica

Tingis
Lixus

Cartennae
Iol
Saldae

Thugga

Carthage (Tunis)

MASAESYLI

Cirta
Zama
202 B.C.

Thapsus

Rusaddir
(Melilla)

NUMIDIA

Theveste

Sala

Capsa

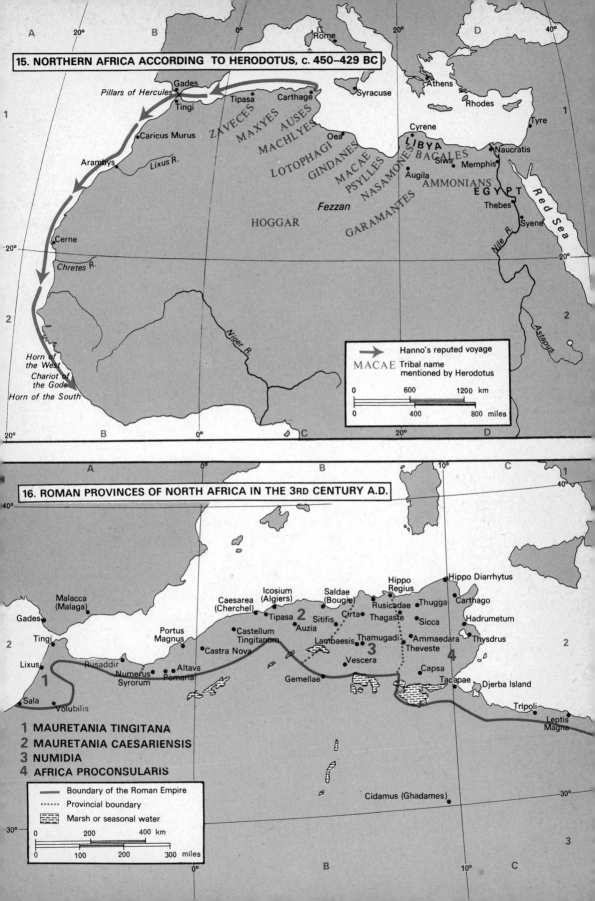

15. NORTHERN AFRICA ACCORDING TO HERODOTUS, c. 450–429 BC

Rome

Pillars of Hercules
Gades
Tingi
Tipasa
Carthage
Syracuse
Athens
Rhodes
Tyre

Caricus Murus
ZAVECES
MAXYES
AUSES
MACHLYES
Cyrene
LIBYA

Arambys
Lixus R.
LOTOPHAGI
GINDANES
Oea
MACAE
Siwa
Memphis
Naucratis

PSYLLES
NASAMONES
BACALES
AMMONIANS
EGYPT

Augila
Thebes
Syene

Fezzan
GARAMANTES

HOGGAR
Nile R.
Red Sea

Cerne

Chretes R.

Niger R.
Astapus

Horn of
the West
Chariot of
the Gods
Horn of the South

→ Hanno's reputed voyage

MACAE Tribal name
mentioned by Herodotus

0   600   1200 km
0   400   800 miles

16. ROMAN PROVINCES OF NORTH AFRICA IN THE 3RD CENTURY A.D.

Malacca
(Malaga)
Gades
Tingi
Lixus
Sala
Volubilis

Rusaddir
Numerus
Syrorum
Pomaria
Altava
Castra Nova

Portus
Magnus
Castellum
Tingitanum

Caesarea
(Cherchel)
Icosium
(Algiers)
Tipasa
Auzia
Sitifis
Saldae
(Bougie)
Cirta
Rusicadae
Hippo
Regius
Hippo Diarrhytus
Thugga
Carthago
Hadrumetum
Thysdrus

Lambaesis
Thamugadi
Thagaste
Sicca
Ammaedara
Theveste
Vescera

Gemellae
Capsa
Tacapae
Djerba Island
Tripoli
Leptis
Magna

Cidamus (Ghadames)

1 MAURETANIA TINGITANA
2 MAURETANIA CAESARIENSIS
3 NUMIDIA
4 AFRICA PROCONSULARIS

—— Boundary of the Roman Empire
······ Provincial boundary
Marsh or seasonal water

0   200   400 km
0   100   200   300 miles

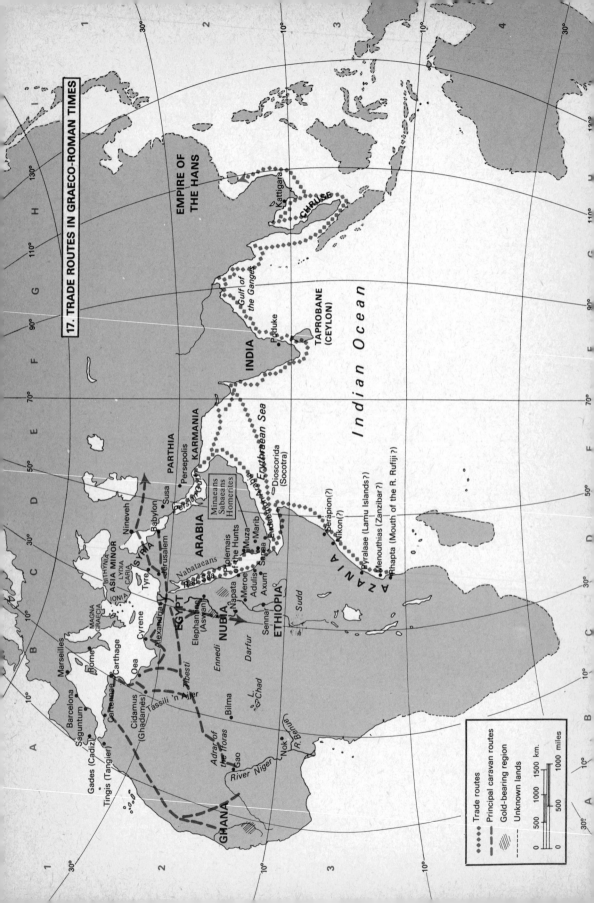

17. TRADE ROUTES IN GRAECO-ROMAN TIMES

EMPIRE OF THE HANS

CHRUSE

Kattigara

INDIA

Gulf of the Ganges

Poduke

TAPROBANE (CEYLON)

Indian Ocean

PARTHIA

KARMANIA

Persepolis

Susa

Nineveh

Babylon

Persian Gulf

ARABIA

Minaeans
Sabaeans
Homerites

SYRIA

Tyre

Jerusalem

Nabataeans

Red Sea

Marib

Ptolemais
of the Hunts

Muza

Erythraean Sea

Dioscorida
(Socotra)

Serapion(?)

Nikon(?)

Pyralaae (Lamu Islands?)

Menouthias (Zanzibar?)

Rhapta (Mouth of the R. Rufiji?)

ASIA MINOR

BITHYNIA
LYDIA
CARIA
IONIA

MAGNA
GRAECIA

Rome

Carthage

Marseilles

Barcelona

Saguntum

Gades (Cadiz)

Tingis (Tangier)

Cirtenae
Carthaeae

Cidamus
(Ghadamès)

Oea

Cyrene

Alexandria

EGYPT

Elephantine
(Aswan)

NUBIA

Napata

Meroe

Adulis

Axum

Sennar

Sudd

ETHIOPIA

Sabea

Darfur

Ennedi

Thesti

Tassili 'n Ajjer

Bilma

L. Chad

Adrar of
the Iforas

Gao

River Niger

Nok

R. Benue

GHANA

AZANIA

Legend:
- Trade routes
- Principal caravan routes
- Gold-bearing region
- Unknown lands

0 500 1000 1500 km.
0 500 1000 miles

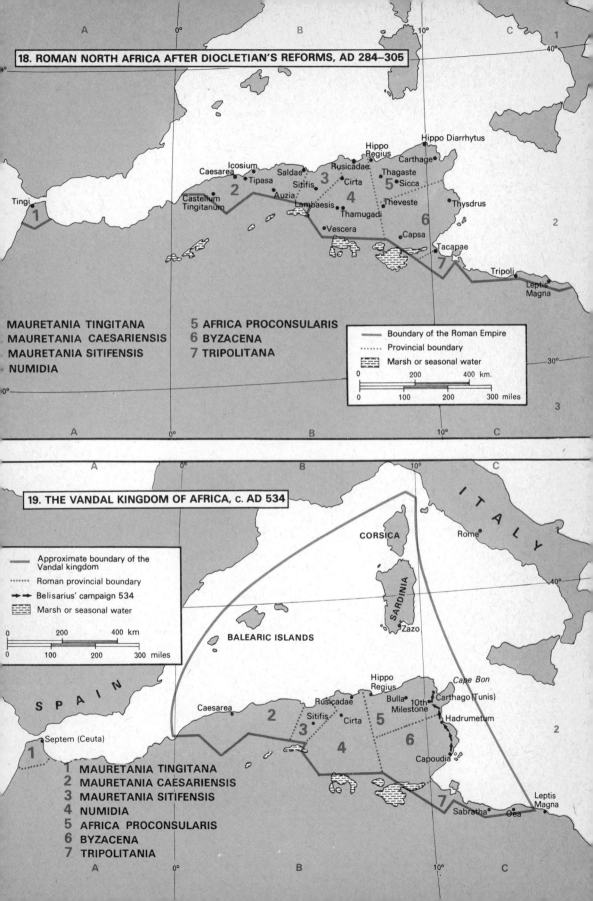

18. ROMAN NORTH AFRICA AFTER DIOCLETIAN'S REFORMS, AD 284–305

Tingi

Castellum Tingitanum

Caesarea
Icosium
Tipasa
Saldae
Sitifis
Auzia
Lambaesis
Vescera
Thamugadi
Rusicadae
Cirta
Hippo Regius
Thagaste
Theveste
Capsa
Hippo Diarrhytus
Carthage
Sicca
Thysdrus
Tacapae
Tripoli
Leptis Magna

1 2 3 4 5 6 7

MAURETANIA TINGITANA
MAURETANIA CAESARIENSIS
MAURETANIA SITIFENSIS
NUMIDIA

5 AFRICA PROCONSULARIS
6 BYZACENA
7 TRIPOLITANA

——— Boundary of the Roman Empire
.... Provincial boundary
Marsh or seasonal water

0   200   400 km.
0   100   200   300 miles

19. THE VANDAL KINGDOM OF AFRICA, c. AD 534

ITALY
CORSICA
Rome
SARDINIA
Zazo
BALEARIC ISLANDS
SPAIN
Septem (Ceuta)
Caesarea
Rusicadae
Sitifis
Cirta
Hippo Regius
Bulla
10th Milestone
Carthago (Tunis)
Cape Bon
Hadrumetum
Capoudia
Leptis Magna
Sabratha
Oea

——— Approximate boundary of the Vandal kingdom
.... Roman provincial boundary
►►► Belisarius' campaign 534
Marsh or seasonal water

0   200   400 km
0   100   200   300 miles

1 MAURETANIA TINGITANA
2 MAURETANIA CAESARIENSIS
3 MAURETANIA SITIFENSIS
4 NUMIDIA
5 AFRICA PROCONSULARIS
6 BYZACENA
7 TRIPOLITANA

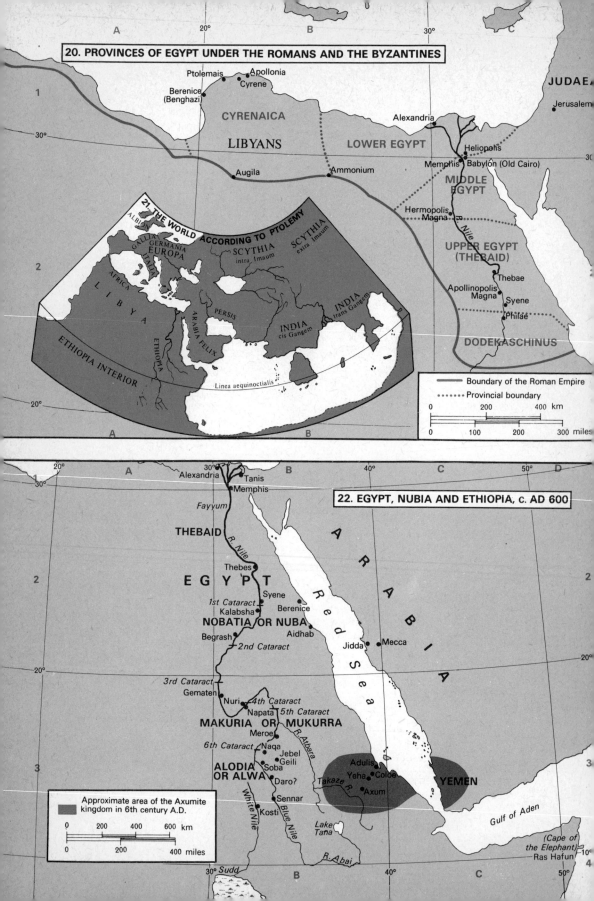

20. PROVINCES OF EGYPT UNDER THE ROMANS AND THE BYZANTINES

A · 20° · B · 30° · C

1

• Ptolemais
• Apollonia
• Cyrene
Berenice •
(Benghazi)

CYRENAICA

LIBYANS

LOWER EGYPT

Alexandria •

JUDAEA

• Jerusalem

30°

30°

• Augila

• Ammonium

Heliopolis
Memphis • • Babylon (Old Cairo)

MIDDLE
EGYPT

21. THE WORLD ACCORDING TO PTOLEMY

ALBION

GERMANIA
GALLIA
EUROPA
ITALIA

SCYTHIA
intra Imaum

SCYTHIA
extra Imaum

Hermopolis
Magna •

UPPER EGYPT
(THEBAID)

2

AFRICA

LIBYA

PERSIS

ARABIA
FELIX

ETHIOPIA

INDIA
cis Gangem

INDIA
trans Gangem

• Thebae
Apollinopolis
Magna • • Syene

• Philae

2

ETHIOPIA INTERIOR

Linea aequinoctialis

DODEKASCHINUS

A · B

20°

20°

———— Boundary of the Roman Empire
· · · · · · Provincial boundary

0   200   400 km
0   100   200   300 miles

22. EGYPT, NUBIA AND ETHIOPIA, c. AD 600

20° · A · 30° · B · 40° · C · 50° · D

1

30°
Alexandria • • Tanis
• Memphis

Fayyum

THEBAID

R. Nile

EGYPT

ARABIA

1

30°

2

Thebes •
Syene •
1st Cataract
Kalabsha •
NOBATIA OR NUBA
• Berenice

Red Sea

2

Begrash •
2nd Cataract
• Aidhab

Jidda • • Mecca

20°

3rd Cataract
Gemeten •
Nuri • 4th Cataract
Napata • 5th Cataract
MAKURIA OR MUKURRA
Meroe •
6th Cataract • Naqa
Jebel
Geili •
Daro? • Soba •
ALODIA
OR ALWA
Sennar •

R. Atbara

Takaze R.

Adulis •
Yeha • • Coloe
• Axum

YEMEN

3

White Nile

Kosti •

Blue Nile

Lake
Tana

R. Abai

Gulf of Aden

(Cape of
the Elephant)
Ras Hafun

10°

■ Approximate area of the Axumite
kingdom in 6th century A.D.

0   200   400   600 km
0   200   400 miles

30° Sudd · B · 40° · C · 50°

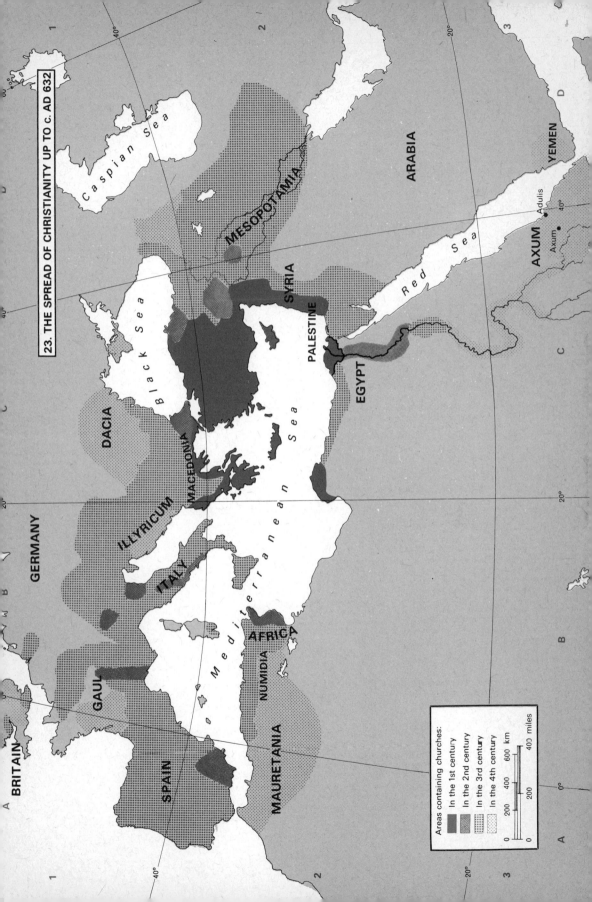

23. THE SPREAD OF CHRISTIANITY UP TO c. AD 632

BRITAIN

GERMANY

GAUL

SPAIN

Caspian Sea

Black Sea

DACIA

ILLYRICUM

MACEDONIA

ITALY

Mediterranean Sea

AFRICA

NUMIDIA

MAURETANIA

MESOPOTAMIA

SYRIA

PALESTINE

EGYPT

Red Sea

ARABIA

YEMEN

AXUM

Adulis

Axum •

Areas containing churches:

In the 1st century

In the 2nd century

In the 3rd century

In the 4th century

600 km

400

200

0

400 miles

200

0

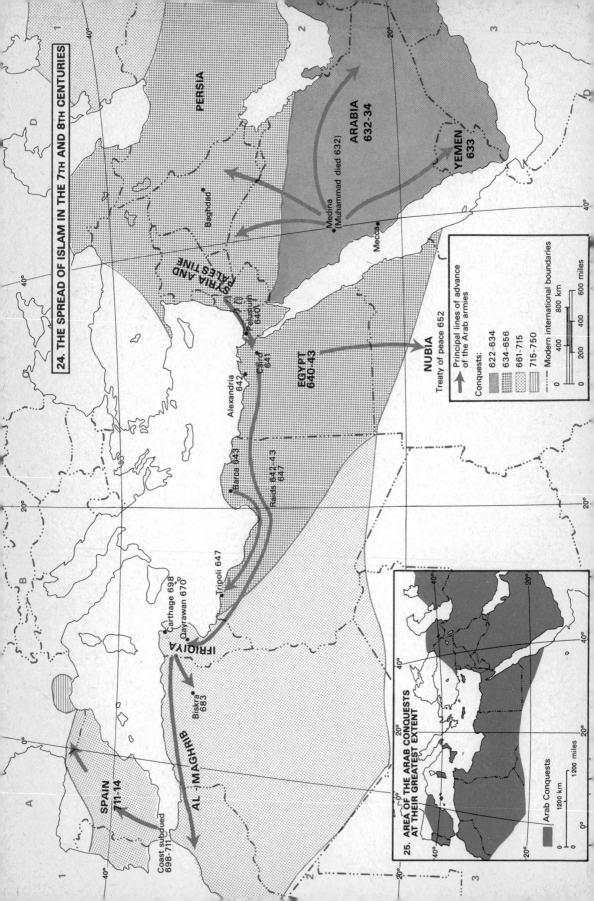

24. THE SPREAD OF ISLAM IN THE 7TH AND 8TH CENTURIES

PERSIA

ARABIA
632-34

Medina
(Muhammad died 632)

YEMEN
633

Mecca

SYRIA AND
PALESTINE

Baghdad

Pelusium
640

Cairo
641

Alexandria
642

EGYPT
640-43

NUBIA

Treaty of peace 652

Berda 643

Raids 642-43,
647

Tripoli 647

Carthage 698

Qayrawan 670

IFRIQIYA

Biskra
683

AL-MAGHRIB

SPAIN
711-14

Coast subdued
698-711

Principal lines of advance
of the Arab armies

Conquests:

622-634

634-656

661-715

715-750

Modern international boundaries

0   400   800 km

0   200   400   600 miles

25. AREA OF THE ARAB CONQUESTS
AT THEIR GREATEST EXTENT

Arab Conquests

0   1200 km

0   1200 miles

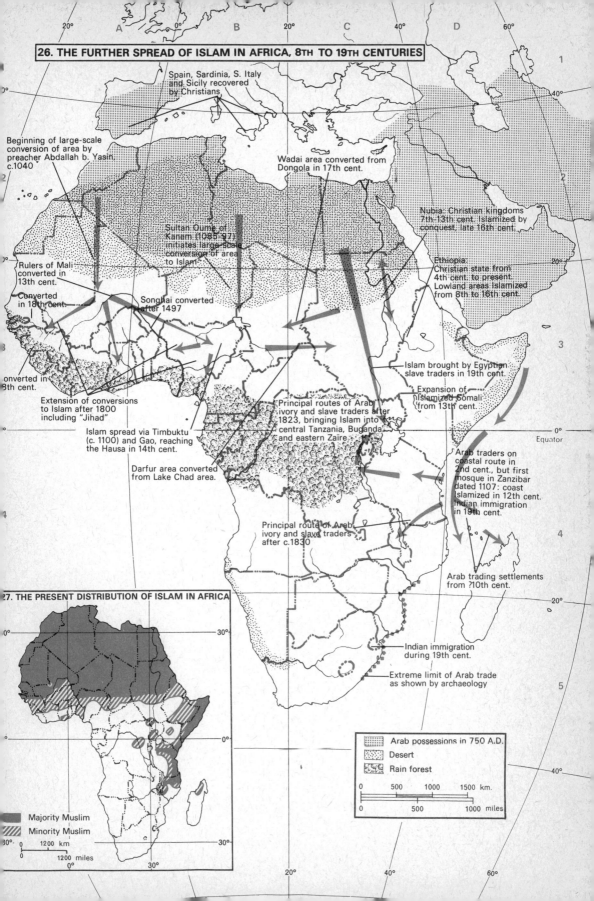

26. THE FURTHER SPREAD OF ISLAM IN AFRICA, 8TH TO 19TH CENTURIES

Spain, Sardinia, S. Italy and Sicily recovered by Christians.

Beginning of large-scale conversion of area by preacher Abdallah b. Yasin, c.1040

Wadai area converted from Dongola in 17th cent.

Nubia: Christian kingdoms 7th-13th cent. Islamized by conquest, late 16th cent.

Sultan Oume of Kanem (1085-97) initiates large-scale conversion of area to Islam.

Rulers of Mali converted in 13th cent.

Ethiopia: Christian state from 4th cent. to present. Lowland areas Islamized from 8th to 16th cent.

Converted in 18th cent.

Songhai converted after 1497

Converted in 8th cent.

Extension of conversions to Islam after 1800 including "Jihad"

Islam brought by Egyptian slave traders in 19th cent.

Expansion of Islamized Somali from 13th cent.

Islam spread via Timbuktu (c. 1100) and Gao, reaching the Hausa in 14th cent.

Principal routes of Arab ivory and slave traders after 1823, bringing Islam into central Tanzania, Buganda and eastern Zaire.

Darfur area converted from Lake Chad area.

Equator

Arab traders on coastal route in 2nd cent., but first mosque in Zanzibar dated 1107: coast Islamized in 12th cent. Indian immigration in 19th cent.

Principal route of Arab ivory and slave traders after c.1830

Arab trading settlements from ?10th cent.

27. THE PRESENT DISTRIBUTION OF ISLAM IN AFRICA

Indian immigration during 19th cent.

Extreme limit of Arab trade as shown by archaeology

Arab possessions in 750 A.D.

Desert

Rain forest

0   500   1000   1500 km.

0   500   1000 miles

Majority Muslim

Minority Muslim

0   1200 km

0   1200 miles

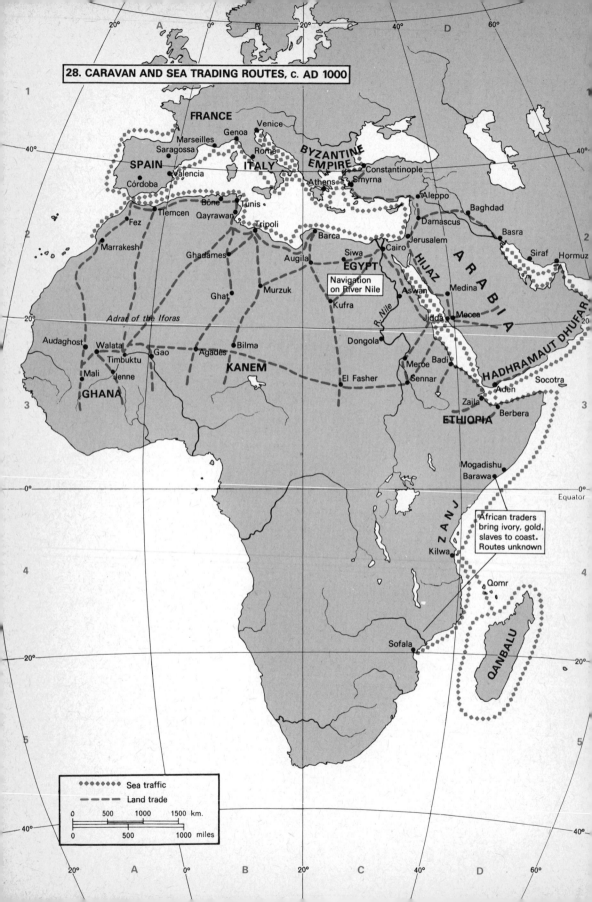

28. CARAVAN AND SEA TRADING ROUTES, c. AD 1000

FRANCE

Venice
Genoa
Marseilles
Saragossa
Rome
SPAIN
Valencia
Córdoba
ITALY
BYZANTINE
EMPIRE
Constantinople
Athens
Smyrna
Aleppo
Baghdad
Bône
Tunis
Tlemcen
Qayrawan
Damascus
Basra
Fez
Tripoli
Barca
Jerusalem
Siraf
Marrakesh
Ghadames
Augila
Siwa
Cairo
Hormuz
EGYPT
Ghat
Murzuk
Kufra
Navigation
on River Nile
Aswan
Medina
ARABIA
HIJAZ
Adrar of the Iforas
Jidda
Mecca
Audaghost
Walata
Gao
Agades
Bilma
Dongola
DHUFAR
HADHRAMAUT
Timbuktu
Mali
Jenne
KANEM
El Fasher
Meroe
Badi
Sennar
Aden
Socotra
GHANA
Zaila
Berbera
ETHIOPIA
R. Nile
Mogadishu
Barawa
Equator
ZANJ
African traders
bring ivory, gold,
slaves to coast.
Routes unknown
Kilwa
Qomr
QANBALU
Sofala

●●●●●●●● Sea traffic
– – – – Land trade

0   500   1000   1500 km.
0   500   1000 miles

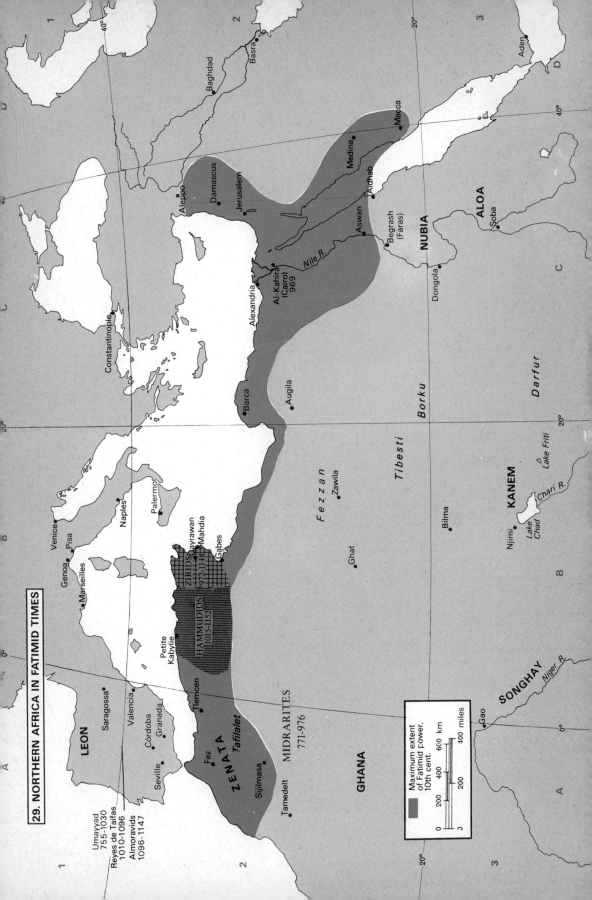

29. NORTHERN AFRICA IN FATIMID TIMES

Umayyad 755-1030
Reyes de Taifas 1010-1096
Almoravids 1096-1147

LEON

Saragossa
Seville
Córdoba
Granada
Valencia

Marseilles
Genoa
Pisa
Venice
Naples
Palermo

Constantinople

Baghdad
Basra

Aleppo
Damascus
Jerusalem
Alexandria
Al-Kahira
(Cairo)
969

Mecca
Medina
'Aidhab
Aswan
Begrash
(Faras)

NUBIA

ALOA
Soba

Dongola

Darfur

Nile R.

Barca
Augila

Fezzan
Zawila
Ghat

Tibesti

Borku

Bilma

KANEM
Njimi
Lake
Chad
Lake Friti
Chari R.

ZIRIDS
972-1148
Kayrawan
Mahdia
Gabes

HAMMUDIDS
1015-1152

Petite
Kabylie

Tlemcen
Fez
ZENATA
Tafilalet
Sijilmasa
Tamedelt

MIDRARITES
771-976

GHANA

SONGHAY
Gao
Niger R.

Aden

Maximum extent
of Fatimid power,
10th cent.

0   200   400   600 km

0   200   400 miles

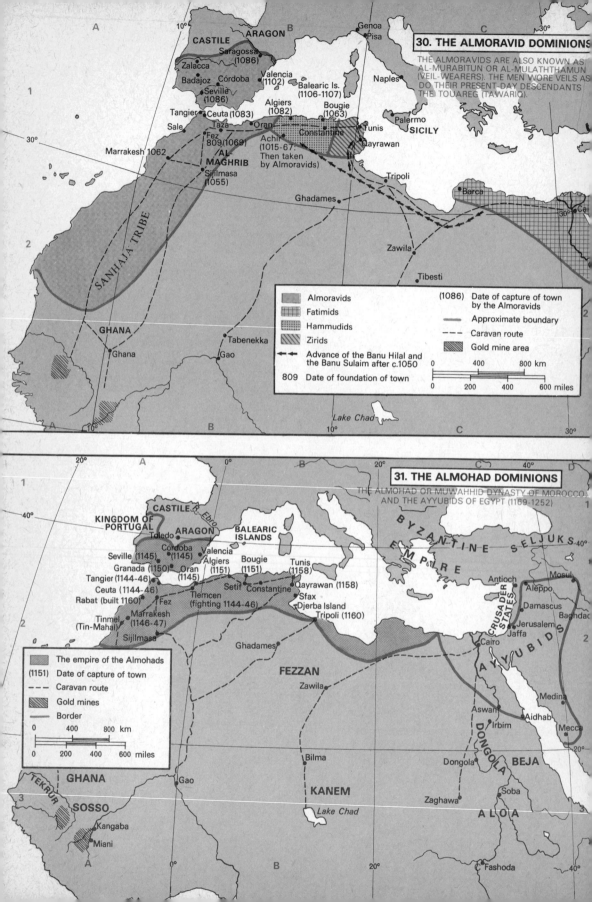

30. THE ALMORAVID DOMINIONS

THE ALMORAVIDS ARE ALSO KNOWN AS
AL-MURABITUN OR AL-MULATHTHAMUN
(VEIL-WEARERS). THE MEN WORE VEILS AS
DO THEIR PRESENT-DAY DESCENDANTS
THE TOUAREG (TAWARIQ).

Genoa
Pisa
CASTILE
ARAGON
Saragossa (1086)
Zalacca
Badajoz Córdoba
Valencia (1102)
Seville (1086)
Balearic Is. (1106-1107)
Naples
Algiers (1082)
Bougie (1063)
Tangier Ceuta (1083)
Sale Taza Oran
Tunis
Palermo
SICILY
Constantine
Qayrawan
Fez 809(1069)
AL MAGHRIB
Achir (1015-67) Then taken by Almoravids)
Marrakesh 1062
Tripoli
Sijilmasa (1055)
Barca
Ghadames
Cai
SANHAJA TRIBE
Zawila
Tibesti
GHANA
Tabenekka
Ghana
Gao
Lake Chad

	Almoravids	(1086)	Date of capture of town by the Almoravids
	Fatimids		Approximate boundary
	Hammudids		Caravan route
	Zirids		Gold mine area

Advance of the Banu Hilal and the Banu Sulaim after c.1050

809 Date of foundation of town

0   400   800 km
0 200 400 600 miles

31. THE ALMOHAD DOMINIONS

THE ALMOHAD OR MUWAHHID DYNASTY OF MOROCCO
AND THE AYYUBIDS OF EGYPT (1169-1252)

KINGDOM OF PORTUGAL
CASTILE
Toledo ARAGON
BALEARIC ISLANDS
Ebro
Cordoba (1145)
Seville (1145)
Valencia
Granada (1150) Algiers (1151)
Bougie (1151)
Tangier (1144-46)
Oran (1145)
Tunis (1158)
Ceuta (1144-46)
Setif Constantine
Qayrawan (1158)
Rabat (built 1160)
Fez
Tlemcen (fighting 1144-46)
Sfax
Djerba Island
Tripoli (1160)
Tinmel (Tin-Mahal)
Marrakesh (1146-47)
Sijilmasa
Ghadames
BYZANTINE EMPIRE
SELJUKS
Antioch
Mosul
Aleppo
Damascus
Baghdad
CRUSADER STATES
Jerusalem
Jaffa
AYYUBIDS
Cairo
FEZZAN
Zawila
Medina
Aswan
Irbim
Aidhab
Mecca
DONGOLA
BEJA

	The empire of the Almohads
(1151)	Date of capture of town
	Caravan route
	Gold mines
	Border

0   400   800 km
0 200 400 600 miles

TEKRUR GHANA
SOSSO
Gao
Bilma
KANEM
Lake Chad
Zaghawa
Dongola
Soba
ALOA
Kangaba
Miani
Fashoda

32. EGYPT AND SYRIA UNDER THE MAMLUKS, 13TH CENTURY TO 1517

Constantinople

30° A   B   40°   C   Tiflis

Trebizond

ARMENIA

TURKS

Caesarea (1277)

Konya   Albistan (1277)   R. Tigris

Sis (sacked 1266, 1275)
Tarsus (sacked 1266)   Adana (sacked 1266)   Edessa

1   Aleppo (1260)   Mosul   1

RHODES   Antioch (1268)   Al-Raqqa

CRETE   Latakia (1287)   Masyal (1270)   R. Euphrates   IL-KHAN
    Tartus   Hama   MONGOLS
    Tripoli (1289)   Homs
    Jubail   (1263)   Palmyra   Baghdad
    Beirut (1291)
    Sidon   Damascus (1260)
    Tyre (1291)
    Acre (1291)   R. Jordan
    Haifa   Busra
    Caesarea (1265)   Nablus
    Jaffa (1268)   Ramla
    Rosetta   Damietta   Ashkelon   Jerusalem (1260)
Alexandria   Gaza   Dead Sea
    El-Arish   Kerak (1263)
30°   (Krak des Chevaliers)   30°
    Cairo   Kutuz and Baybars
    1259-77

El-Fayyum

2   Medina   2

1st Cataract   Aswan   Yanbu

Red
Sea

2nd Cataract

NUBIA   AL-HIJAZ

20°   Jidda   Mecca   20°

3rd Cataract

Dongola

4th   Suakin
Cataract   5th Cataract

(1291) Date of battle

Egypt proper

Area recovered from the Crusaders

Tributary to the Mamluks

6th Cataract

0   200   400 km

0   100   200   300 miles

3   A   B   C   3
30°   40°

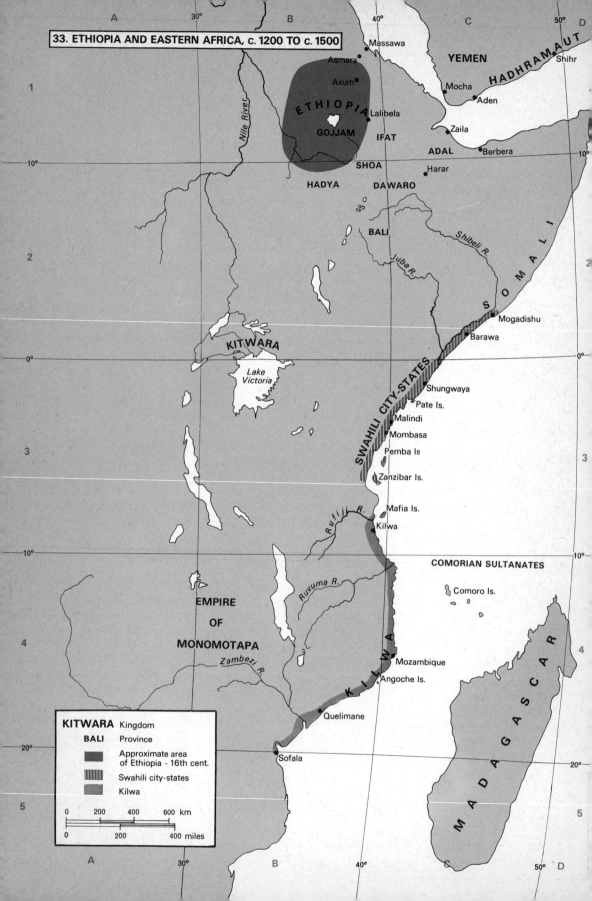

33. ETHIOPIA AND EASTERN AFRICA, c. 1200 TO c. 1500

A · 30° · B · 40° · C · 50° · D

Massawa

YEMEN · **HADHRAMAUT**

Asmara · Shihr

Axum · Mocha

1 · Aden · 1

Nile River

E T H I O P I A · Lalibela · Zaila

GOJJAM · IFAT

ADAL · Berbera

10° · SHOA · 10°

HADYA · DAWARO · Harar

BALI

Shibeli R.

2 · S O M A L I · 2

Juba R.

Mogadishu

Barawa

0° · KITWARA · Shungwaya · 0°

Lake Victoria · Pate Is.

Malindi

Mombasa

3 · Pemba Is · 3

Zanzibar Is.

Rufiji R. · Mafia Is.

Kilwa

10° · **COMORIAN SULTANATES** · 10°

Ruvuma R. · Comoro Is.

EMPIRE

OF

MONOMOTAPA · K I L W A

Zambezi R. · Mozambique

4 · Angoche Is. · 4

Quelimane

M A D A G A S C A R

20° · Sofala · 20°

KITWARA Kingdom

BALI Province

Approximate area
of Ethiopia – 16th cent.

Swahili city-states

Kilwa

0   200   400   600 km

0   200   400 miles

A · 30° · B · 40° · C · 50° · D

SWAHILI CITY STATES

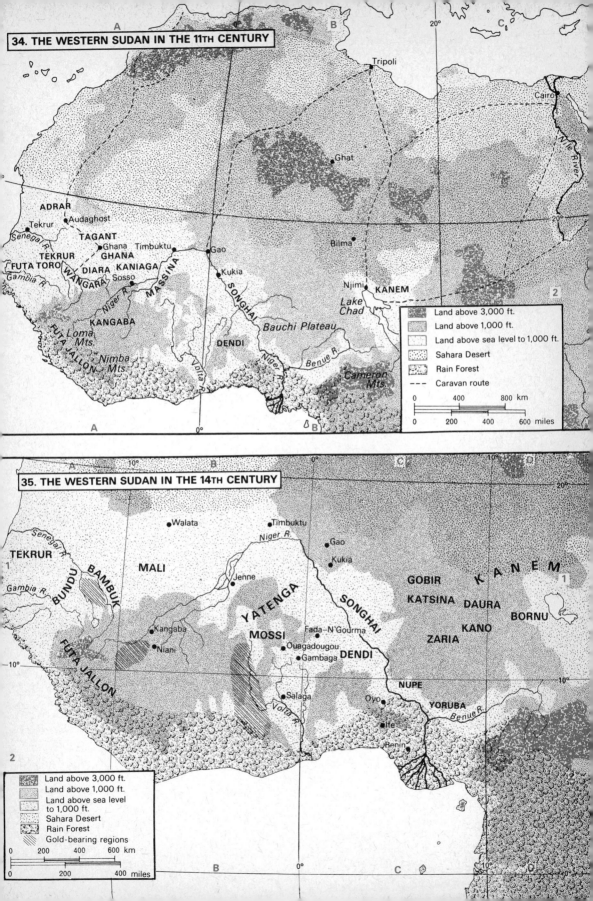

34. THE WESTERN SUDAN IN THE 11TH CENTURY

A   0°   B   20°   C

Tripoli

Cairo

Ghat

Nile River

ADRAR

Tekrur   Audaghost

TAGANT

Ghana   Timbuktu   Gao

TEKRUR   GHANA

FUTA TORO   DIARA   KANIAGA

Senegal R.

WANGARA   Sosso

Gambia R.   Niger R.   MASSINA

Kukia

Bilma

Njimi   KANEM

Lake Chad

SONGHAI

KANGABA

Loma Mts.

FUTA JALLON

Nimba Mts.

DENDI

Bauchi Plateau

Niger R.

Volta R.

Benue R.

Cameroon Mts.

20°

2

▨	Land above 3,000 ft.
▦	Land above 1,000 ft.
□	Land above sea level to 1,000 ft.
⋮	Sahara Desert
▨	Rain Forest
---	Caravan route

0   400   800 km

0   200   400   600 miles

A   0°   B

35. THE WESTERN SUDAN IN THE 14TH CENTURY

A   10°   B   0°   C   10°   D

20°

TEKRUR

Senegal R.

Walata

Timbuktu

Niger R.

Gao

Kukia

1

Gambia R.

BUNDU   BAMBUK

MALI

Jenne

GOBIR

KATSINA   DAURA

KANEM

BORNU

FUTA JALLON

Kangaba

Niani

YATENGA

MOSSI

Fada-N'Gourma

Ouagadougou

Gambaga

SONGHAI

DENDI

ZARIA

KANO

10°

Salaga

Volta R.

NUPE

Oyo

YORUBA

Benue R.

Ife

Benin

10°

2

▨	Land above 3,000 ft.
▦	Land above 1,000 ft.
□	Land above sea level to 1,000 ft.
⋮	Sahara Desert
▨	Rain Forest
▥	Gold-bearing regions

0   200   400   600 km

0   200   400 miles

B   0°   C

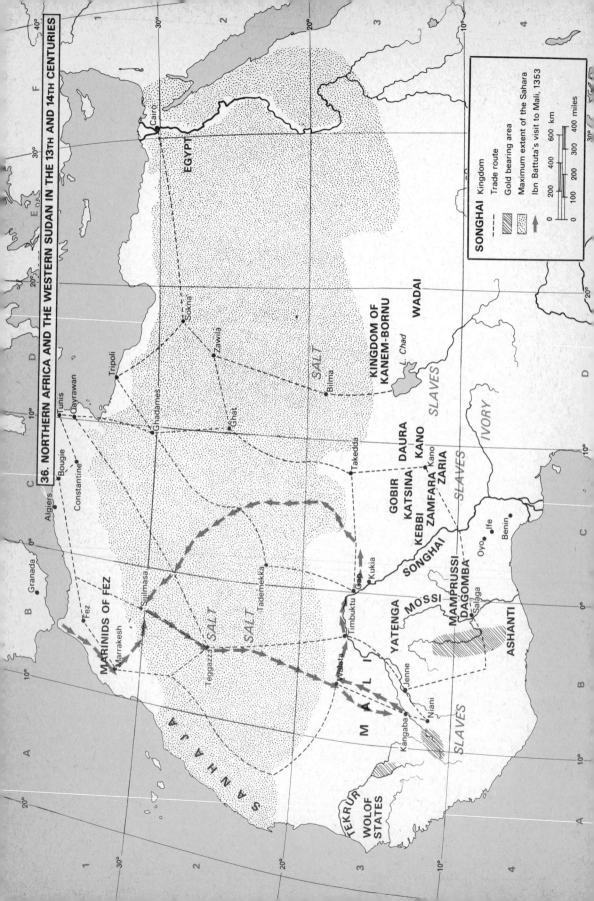

36. NORTHERN AFRICA AND THE WESTERN SUDAN IN THE 13TH AND 14TH CENTURIES

SONGHAI Kingdom
- - - Trade route
Gold bearing area
Maximum extent of the Sahara
Ibn Battuta's visit to Mali, 1353

0 200   400   600 km
0 100 200 300 400 miles

Granada

Algiers
Bougie
Constantine
Tunis
Qayrawan
Tripoli
Sokna
Cairo

EGYPT

Fez
MARINIDS OF FEZ
Marrakesh
Sijilmasa
Ghadames
Zawila
Ghat
Bilma

KINGDOM OF
KANEM-BORNU

WADAI

S A N H A J A
Teggazza
SALT
SALT
SALT
Tademekka
Takedda
L. Chad

SALT

SLAVES

TEKRUR
WOLOF
STATES

M A L I
Walata
Timbuktu
Gao
Kukia

GOBIR
KATSINA
KEBBI
ZAMFARA
ZARIA
DAURA
KANO
Kano

SLAVES

IVORY

Niani
Kangaba
Jenne
YATENGA
MOSSI
SONGHAI
MAMPRUSSI
DAGOMBA
Salaga
Oyo
Ife
Benin
ASHANTI

SLAVES

SLAVES

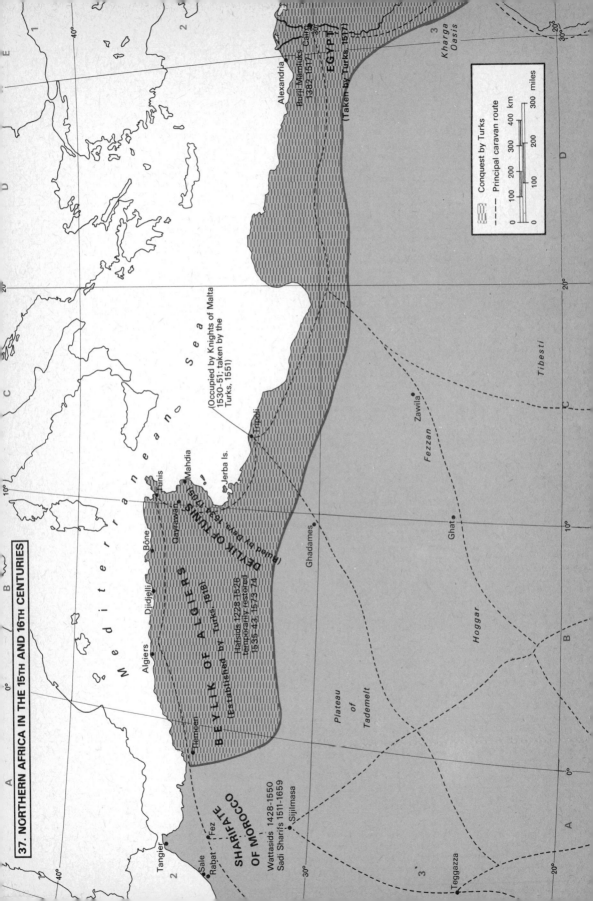

37. NORTHERN AFRICA IN THE 15TH AND 16TH CENTURIES

Mediterranean Sea

Tangier
Sale
Rabat
Fez

**SHARIFATE
OF MOROCCO**

Wattasids 1428-1550
Sadi Sharifs 1511-1659

Sijilmasa

Teggazza

Tlemcen

Algiers
Djidjelli
Bône
Qayrawan

BEYLIK OF ALGIERS
(Established by Turks, 1518)

Tunis
Mahdia
Jerba Is.

DEYLIK OF TUNIS

Hafsids 1228-1526
temporarily restored
1535-43, 1573-74
(taken by beys 1534, 1569)

Tripoli

(Occupied by Knights of Malta
1530-51; taken by the
Turks, 1551)

Ghadames

Ghat

Fezzan

Zawila

Alexandria
Cairo
Burji Mamluks
1382-1517

EGYPT

(Taken by Turks, 1517)

Kharga
Oasis

Plateau
of
Tademelt

Hoggar

Tibesti

Conquest by Turks
Principal caravan route

0   100   200   300   400 km
0   100   200   300 miles

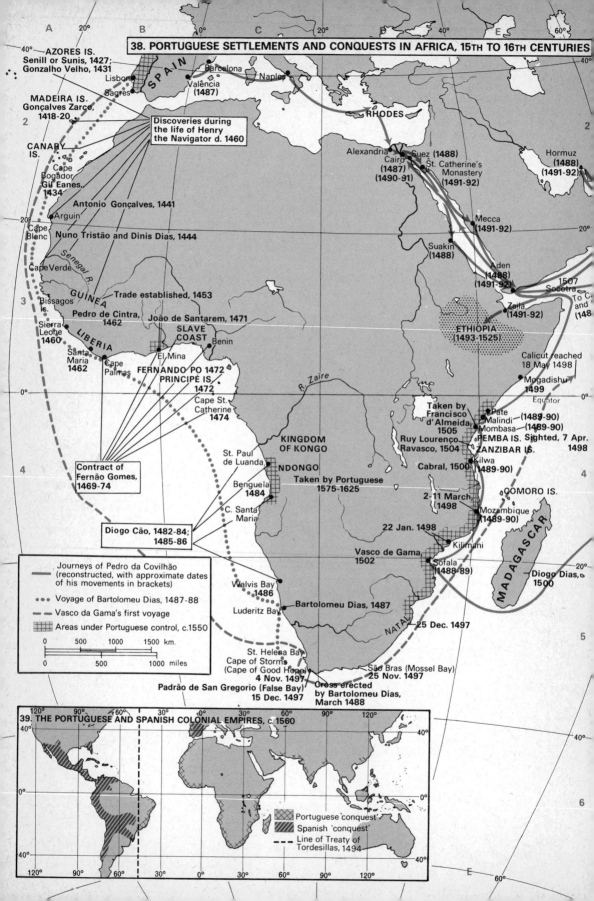

38. PORTUGUESE SETTLEMENTS AND CONQUESTS IN AFRICA, 15TH TO 16TH CENTURIES

AZORES IS.
Senill or Sunis, 1427;
Gonzalho Velho, 1431

Barcelona

SPAIN

Lisbon
València
(1487)

Naples

Sagres

MADEIRA IS.
Gonçalves Zarco,
1418-20

RHODES

Discoveries during
the life of Henry
the Navigator d. 1460

Alexandria
Cairo
(1487)
(1490-91)
Suez (1488)
St. Catherine's
Monastery
(1491-92)

Hormuz
(1488)
(1491-92)

CANARY
IS.

Cape
Bogador
Gil Eanes,
1434

Mecca
(1491-92)

Arguin

Antonio Gonçalves, 1441

Cape
Blanc

Nuno Tristão and Dinis Dias, 1444

Suakin
(1488)

Senegal R.

Aden
(1488)
(1491-92)

1507
Socotra
To C.
and
(148

Cape Verde

GUINEA

Zaila
(1491-92)

Bissagos
Is.

Trade established, 1453

Pedro de Cintra,
1462

João de Santarem, 1471

Sierra
Leone
1460

LIBERIA

SLAVE
COAST

Benin

ETHIOPIA
(1493-1525)

Calicut reached
18 May 1498

Santa
Maria
1462

Cape
Palmas

El Mina

FERNANDO PO 1472
PRINCIPÉ IS.
1472

R. Zaïre

Equator

Mogadishu
1499

Cape St.
Catherine
1474

Pate
Taken by
Francisco
d'Almeida,
1505

Malindi
(1489-90)
(1489-90)

Mombasa
PEMBA IS. Sighted, 7 Apr.
1498

St. Paul
de Luanda

KINGDOM
OF KONGO

Ruy Lourenço
Ravasco, 1504

ZANZIBAR IS.

Contract of
Fernão Gomes,
1469-74

NDONGO

Taken by Portuguese
1575-1625

Kilwa
Cabral, 1500
(1489-90)

Benguela
1484

C. Santa
Maria

COMORO IS.

2-11 March,
1498

Mozambique
(1489-90)

Diogo Cão, 1482-84;
1485-86

22 Jan. 1498

Kilimani

Vasco de Gama,
1502

Sofala
(1488-89)

Diogo Dias,
1500

NATAL

25 Dec. 1497

0   500   1000   1500 km.

0   500   1000 miles

Walvis Bay
1486

Bartolomeu Dias, 1487

Luderitz Bay

St. Helena Bay
Cape of Storms
(Cape of Good Hope)
4 Nov. 1497

São Bras (Mossel Bay)
25 Nov. 1497

Padrão de San Gregorio (False Bay)
15 Dec. 1497

Cross erected
by Bartolomeu Dias,
March 1488

MADAGASCAR

39. THE PORTUGUESE AND SPANISH COLONIAL EMPIRES, c. 1560

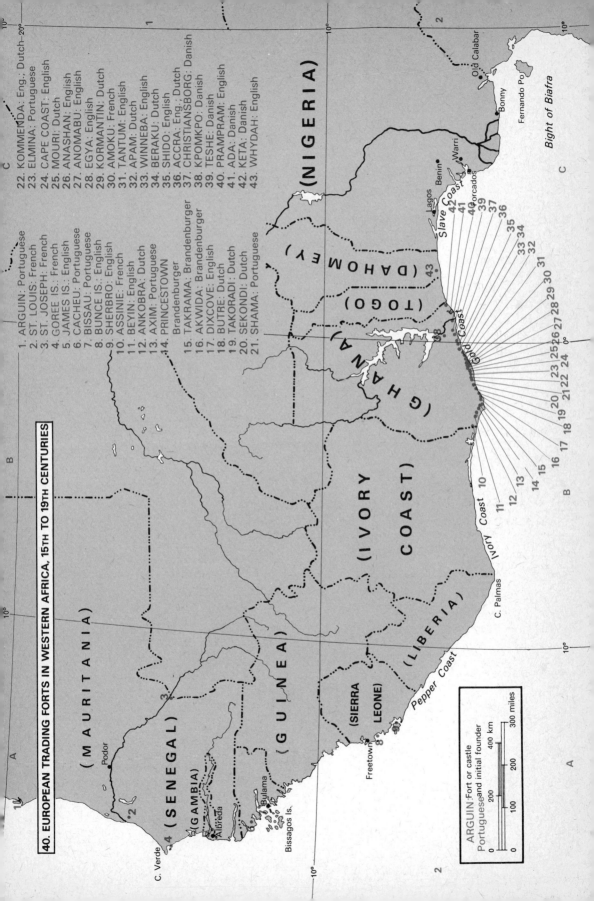

40. EUROPEAN TRADING FORTS IN WESTERN AFRICA, 15TH TO 19TH CENTURIES

1. ARGUIN: Portuguese
2. ST. LOUIS: French
3. ST. JOSEPH: French
4. GOREE IS.: French
5. JAMES IS.: English
6. CACHEU: Portuguese
7. BISSAU: Portuguese
8. BUNCE IS.: English
9. SHERBRO: English
10. ASSINIE: French
11. BEYIN: English
12. ANKOBRA: Dutch
13. AXIM: Portuguese
14. PRINCESTOWN
    Brandenburger
15. TAKRAMA: Brandenburger
16. AKWIDA: Brandenburger
17. DIXCOVE: English
18. BUTRE: Dutch
19. TAKORADI: Dutch
20. SEKONDI: Dutch
21. SHAMA: Portuguese

22. KOMMENDA: Eng.; Dutch–20-
23. ELMINA: Portuguese
24. CAPE COAST: English
25. MOURI: Dutch
26. ANASHAN: English
27. ANOMABU: English
28. EGYA: English
29. KORMANTIN: Dutch
30. AMOKU: French
31. TANTUM: English
32. APAM: Dutch
33. WINNEBA: English
34. BERAKU: Dutch
35. SHIDO: English
36. ACCRA: Eng.; Dutch
37. CHRISTIANSBORG: Danish
38. KPOMKPO: Danish
39. TESHE: Danish
40. PRAMPRAM: English
41. ADA: Danish
42. KETA: Danish
43. WHYDAH: English

ARGUIN–Fort or castle
Portuguese·and initial founder

0   100   200   300 miles
0 200 400 km

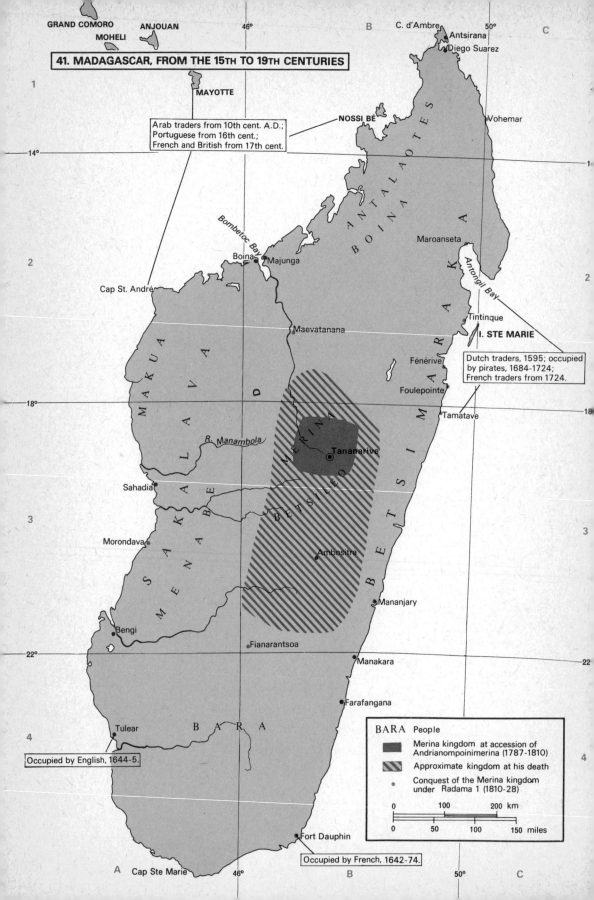

41. MADAGASCAR, FROM THE 15TH TO 19TH CENTURIES

GRAND COMORO   ANJOUAN

MOHELI

MAYOTTE

C. d'Ambre

Antsirana

Diego Suarez

NOSSI BÉ

Arab traders from 10th cent. A.D.;
Portuguese from 16th cent.;
French and British from 17th cent.

Vohemar

A N T A L A O T E S

B O I N A

Bombetoc Bay

Boina Majunga

Cap St. André

Maroanseta

Antongil Bay

Tintinque

I. STE MARIE

Maevatanana

Fénérive

Foulepointe

Dutch traders, 1595; occupied
by pirates, 1684-1724;
French traders from 1724.

M A K U A

S A K A L A V A

M A D I

MERINA

R. Manambola

Tananarive

Tamatave

B E T S I L E O

B E T S I M A R A K A

Sahadia

M E N A B E

Morondava

Ambositre

Mananjary

Bengi

Fianarantsoa

Manakara

22°

Farafangana

B A R A

Tulear

Occupied by English, 1644-5.

BARA People

Merina kingdom at accession of
Andrianompoinimerina (1787-1810)

Approximate kingdom at his death

Conquest of the Merina kingdom
under Radama 1 (1810-28)

0   100   200 km

0   50   100   150 miles

Fort Dauphin

Cap Ste Marie

Occupied by French, 1642-74.

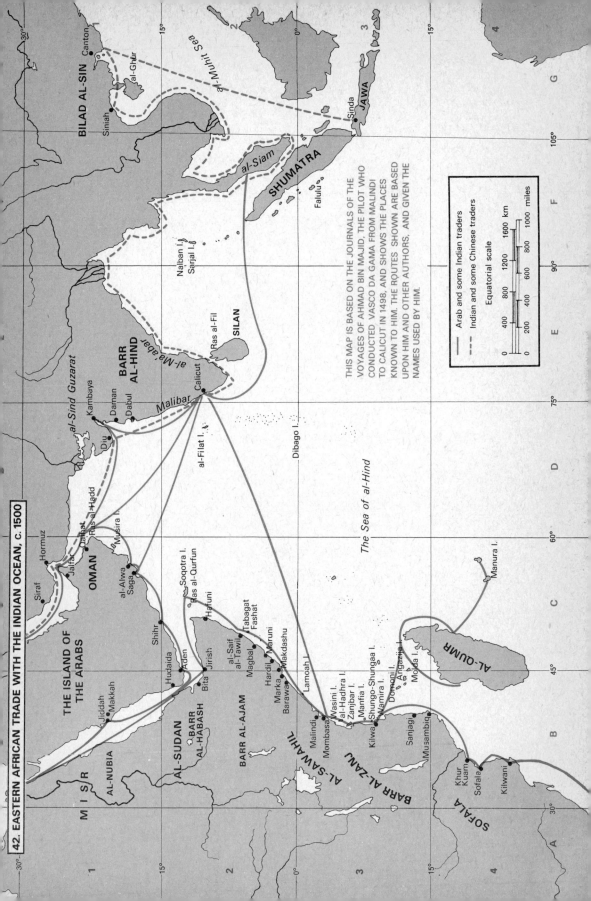

42. EASTERN AFRICAN TRADE WITH THE INDIAN OCEAN, C. 1500

THIS MAP IS BASED ON THE JOURNALS OF THE
VOYAGES OF AHMAD BIN MAJID, THE PILOT WHO
CONDUCTED VASCO DA GAMA FROM MALINDI
TO CALICUT IN 1498, AND SHOWS THE PLACES
KNOWN TO HIM. THE ROUTES SHOWN ARE BASED
UPON HIM AND OTHER AUTHORS, AND GIVEN THE
NAMES USED BY HIM.

———— Arab and some Indian traders

- - - - Indian and some Chinese traders

Equatorial scale

0 400   800   1200   1600 km
0   200   400   600   800   1000 miles

The Sea of al-Hind

BILAD AL-SIN
Canton
al-Ghur
Siniah
al-Muhit Sea

al-Siam

SHUMATRA
Falulu
JAWA
Sinda

Naiban I.
Sarjal I.

SILAN
Ras al-Fil

al-Ma'abar

BARR
AL-HIND
Malibar
Calicut

al-Sind Guzarat
Kambaya
Daman
Dabul
Diu

al-Filat I.

Dibago I.

THE ISLAND OF
THE ARABS

Siraf
Hormuz
Jalfar
Dalhat
Ras al-Hadd
Musira I.

OMAN
al-Alwa
Saga

Soqotra I.
Ras al-Qurfun

Hafuni

MISR
Jiddah
Makkah

AL-NUBIA

AL-SUDAN
Hudaida
Shihr
Aden
Jirish
Bita

BARR
AL-HABASH

BARR AL-AJAM

Tabagat
Fashat
al-Saif
al-Tawil
Magbal
Maruni
Hardi
Marka
Makdashu
Barawa
Lamoah I.

AL-SAWAHIL

BARR AL-ZANJ

Malindi
Mombasa
Wasini I.
al-Hadhra I.
Zanjbar I.
Manfia I.
Kilwa
Shungo-Shungaa I.
Wamira I.
Domoni I.
Angazija I.
Moda I.

AL-QUMR

Manura I.

Sanjagi
Musambiq

SOFALA
Khur
Kuam
Sofala
Kilwani

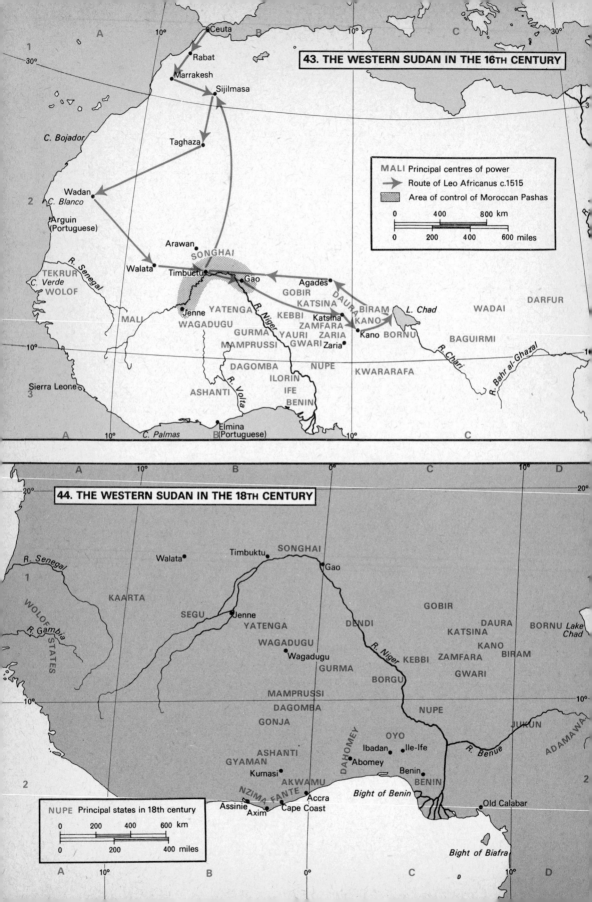

43. THE WESTERN SUDAN IN THE 16TH CENTURY

Ceuta
Rabat
Marrakesh
Sijilmasa

C. Bojador

Taghaza

C. Blanco
Wadan

Arguin
(Portuguese)

Arawan

ARAWAN
SONGHAI
Walata
Timbuctu
Gao
Agades

R. Senegal
TEKRUR
C. Verde
WOLOF

MALI
Jenne
YATENGA
WAGADUGU
GURMA
MAMPRUSSI

GOBIR
KATSINA
DAURA
BIRAM
L. Chad
KEBBI
ZAMFARA
Katsina
KANO
YAURI ZARIA
Kano BORNU
GWARI
Zaria

WADAI
DARFUR

BAGUIRMI
R. Chari
R. Bahr al-Ghazal

DAGOMBA
NUPE
KWARARAFA

Sierra Leone

R. Volta
ASHANTI
ILORIN
IFE
BENIN

C. Palmas
Elmina
(Portuguese)

MALI Principal centres of power

→ Route of Leo Africanus c.1515

▨ Area of control of Moroccan Pashas

0   400   800 km
0   200   400   600 miles

44. THE WESTERN SUDAN IN THE 18TH CENTURY

R. Senegal

WOLOF

R. Gambia
STATES

KAARTA

Walata
Timbuktu
SONGHAI
Gao

SEGU
Jenne
YATENGA
WAGADUGU
Wagadugu
GURMA

DENDI

R. Niger
KEBBI

GOBIR

KATSINA
DAURA
BORNU Lake
Chad
KANO
ZAMFARA
BIRAM
GWARI

BORGU

NUPE
JUKUN

MAMPRUSSI
DAGOMBA
GONJA

ASHANTI
GYAMAN
Kumasi
AKWAMU
NZIMA FANTE
Assinie Axim Cape Coast
Accra

DAHOMEY
Abomey
OYO
Ibadan Ile-Ife

Benin
BENIN

ADAMAWA

R. Benue

Old Calabar

Bight of Benin

Bight of Biafra

NUPE Principal states in 18th century

0   200   400   600 km
0   200   400 miles

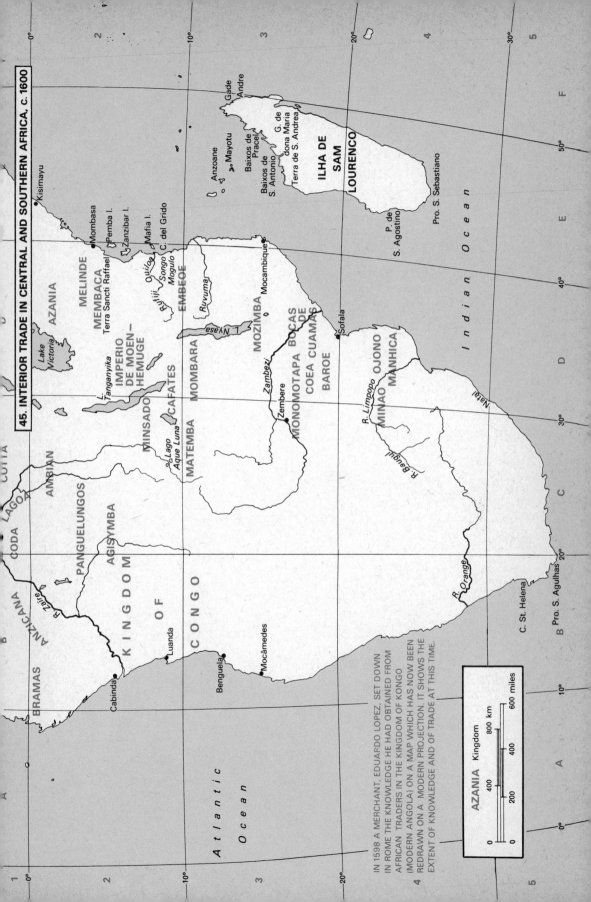

45. INTERIOR TRADE IN CENTRAL AND SOUTHERN AFRICA, C. 1600

IN 1598 A MERCHANT, EDUARDO LOPEZ, SET DOWN
IN ROME THE KNOWLEDGE HE HAD OBTAINED FROM
AFRICAN TRADERS IN THE KINGDOM OF KONGO
(MODERN ANGOLA) ON A MAP WHICH HAS NOW BEEN
REDRAWN ON A MODERN PROJECTION. IT SHOWS THE
EXTENT OF KNOWLEDGE AND OF TRADE AT THIS TIME.

AZANIA Kingdom

Scale:
0   400   800 km
0   200   400   600 miles

Atlantic Ocean

Indian Ocean

BRAMAS
ANZICANA
CODA
LAGOA
CUTTA
AMBIAN
PANGUELUNGOS
AGISYMBA
KINGDOM
OF
CONGO
Cabinda
Luanda
Benguela
Mocâmedes
R. Zaire

AZANIA
Lake Victoria
L. Tanganyika
IMPERIO DE MOEN– HEMUGE
MINSADO
CAFATES
MATEMBA
Lago Aque Luna
MOMBARA
EMBEOE
MELINDE
MEMBACA
Terra Sancti Raffael
Mombasa
Pemba I.
Zanzibar I.
Mafia I.
C. del Grido
Quiloa
Bufiii
Songo
Mogulo
Ruvuma
L. Nyasa
MOZIMBA
Mocambique
Zambezi
Zembere
MONOMOTAPA
BOCAS DE CUAMAS
COEA
BAROE
Sofala
MINAO OJONO
MANHICA
R. Limpopo
R. Baugul
R. Orange
Natal
C. St. Helena
Pro. S. Agulhas
Kisimayu

Anzoane
Mayotu
Baixos de Pracel
Baixos de S. Antonio
G. de Dona Maria
Terra de S. Andrea
Gâde
Andre
ILHA DE SAM LOURENCO
P. de S. Agostino
Pro. S. Sebastiano

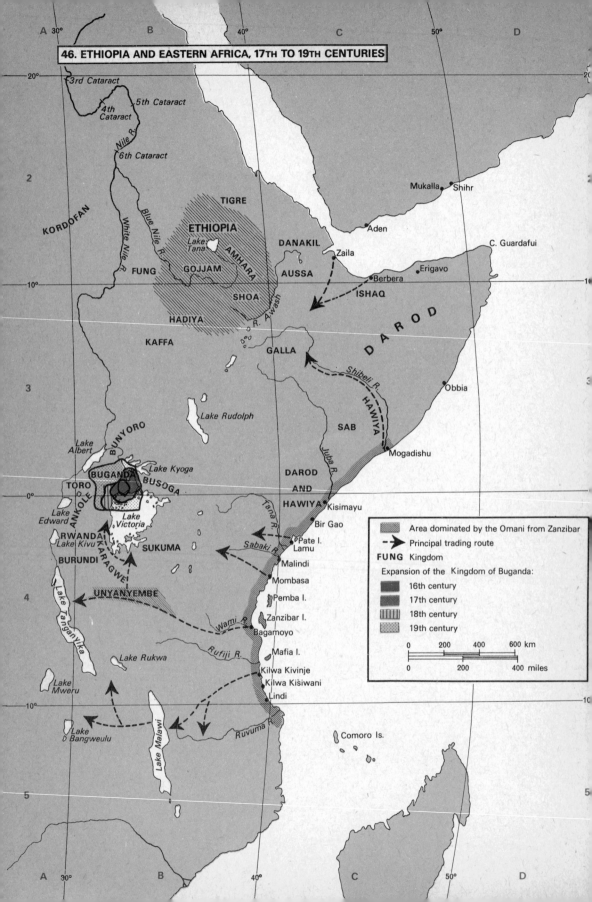

46. ETHIOPIA AND EASTERN AFRICA, 17TH TO 19TH CENTURIES

3rd Cataract

5th Cataract

4th Cataract

Nile R.

6th Cataract

KORDOFAN

White Nile R.

Blue Nile R.

FUNG

TIGRE

ETHIOPIA

Lake Tana

AMHARA

GOJJAM

SHOA

HADIYA

KAFFA

DANAKIL

AUSSA

Zaila

Mukalla · Shihr

· Aden

Berbera

Erigavo

C. Guardafui

ISHAQ

D A R O D

R. Awash

GALLA

Shibeli R.

· Obbia

HAWIYA

Lake Rudolph

SAB

Juba R.

Mogadishu

Lake Albert

BUNYORO

BUGANDA

Lake Kyoga

TORO

BUSOGA

ANKOLE

Lake Edward

Lake Victoria

RWANDA

Lake Kivu

KARAGWE

BURUNDI

SUKUMA

UNYANYEMBE

Lake Tanganyika

DAROD

AND

HAWIYA

Kisimayu

Bir Gao

Tana R.

Pate I.

Lamu

Sabaki R.

Malindi

Mombasa

Pemba I.

Zanzibar I.

Wami R.

Bagamoyo

Lake Rukwa

Rufiji R.

Mafia I.

Kilwa Kivinje

Kilwa Kisiwani

Lindi

Lake Mweru

Lake Bangweulu

Lake Malawi

Ruvuma R.

Comoro Is.

	Area dominated by the Omani from Zanzibar
- - ➤	Principal trading route
FUNG	Kingdom

Expansion of the Kingdom of Buganda:

16th century

17th century

18th century

19th century

0 200 400 600 km

0 200 400 miles

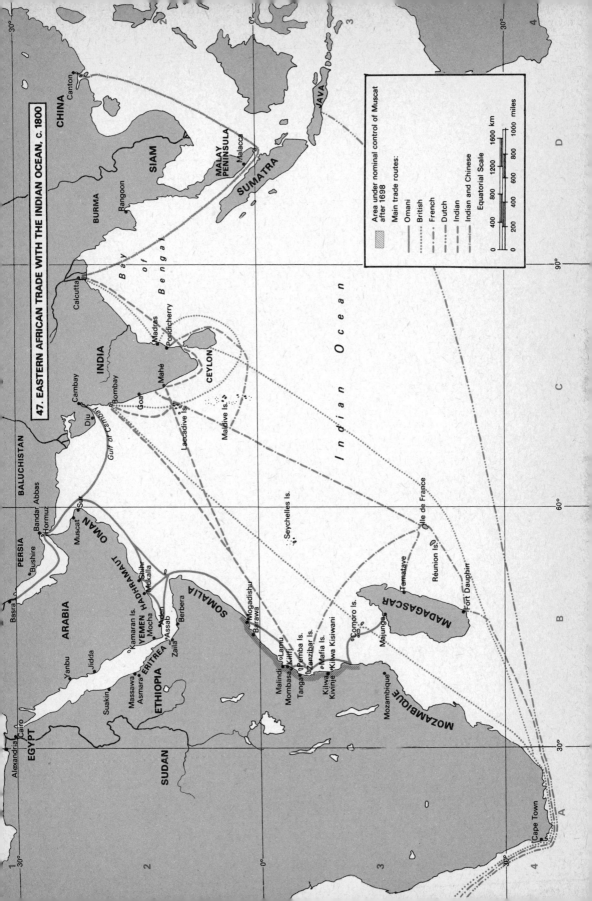

47. EASTERN AFRICAN TRADE WITH THE INDIAN OCEAN. C. 1800

Area under nominal control of Muscat after 1698

Main trade routes:
Omani
British
French
Dutch
Indian
Indian and Chinese

Equatorial Scale

0   200   400   600   800   1000   miles
0   400   800   1200   1600 km

EGYPT
Alexandria
Cairo
SUDAN
Suakin
Yanbu
Jidda
Massawa
Asmara
ETHIOPIA
ERITREA
Zaila
Berbera
ARABIA
Basra
Bushire
Bandar Abbas
Hormuz
PERSIA
BALUCHISTAN
Sur
Muscat
OMAN
Shihr
Mukalla
HADHRAMAUT
Aden
Mocha
YEMEN
Kamaran Is.
SOMALIA
Mogadishu
Barawa
Malindi
Mombasa
Lamu
Kilifi
Tanga
Pemba Is.
Zanzibar Is.
Mafia Is.
Kilwa Kisiwani
Kilwa Kivinje
Comoro Is.
Majunga
MADAGASCAR
Mozambique
MOZAMBIQUE
Trematave
Réunion Is.
Ile de France
Fort Dauphin
Seychelles Is.
Cape Town

Indian Ocean

INDIA
Cambay
Gulf of Cambay
Diu
Bombay
Goa
Mahé
Laccadive Is.
Maldive Is.
CEYLON
Madras
Pondicherry
Calcutta
Bay of Bengal
BURMA
Rangoon
SIAM
CHINA
Canton
MALAY PENINSULA
Malacca
SUMATRA
JAVA

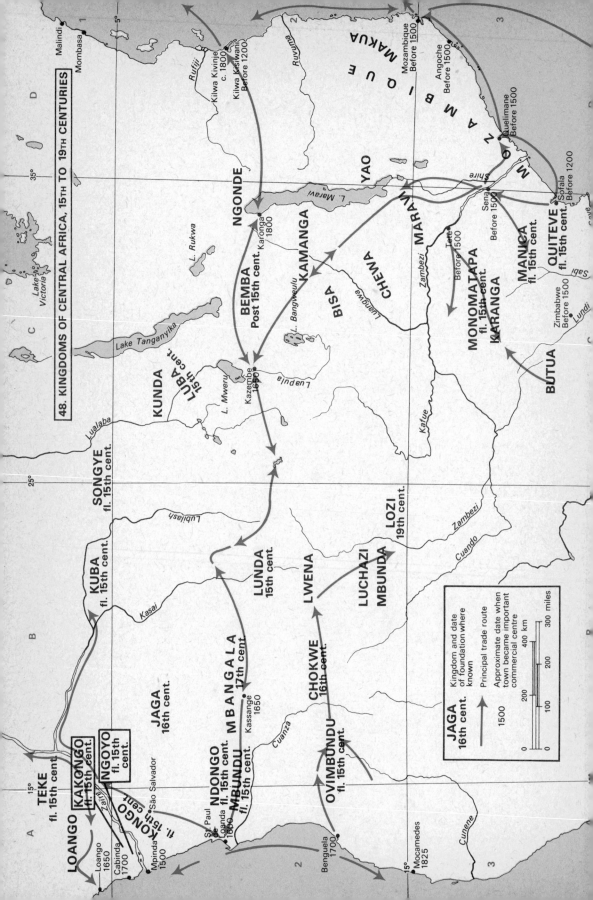

48. KINGDOMS OF CENTRAL AFRICA, 15TH TO 19TH CENTURIES

Malindi
Mombasa

Kilwa Kivinje c. 1800
Kilwa Kisiwani Before 1200

Rufiji
Ruvuma

MOZAMBIQUE

Mozambique Before 1500
Angoche Before 1500
Quelimane Before 1500

MAKUA

NGONDE

Karonga 1800

L. Marawi

YAO

BEMBA Post 15th cent.

KAMANGA

Shire
Sena Before 1500

Sofala Before 1200

QUITEVE fl. 15th cent.

L. Rukwa

Kazembe 1650

Luapula

BISA

CHEWA

MARAVI

Tete Before 1500

Zambezi

MANICA fl. 15th cent.

Lake Victoria

Lake Tanganyika

KUNDA

LUBA 15th cent.

L. Mweru

L. Bangweulu

MONOMATAPA fl. 15th cent.

KARANGA

BUTUA

Zimbabwe Before 1500

Lundi

Sabi

Luangwa

Kafue

Lualaba

SONGYE fl. 15th cent.

Lubilash

KUBA fl. 15th cent.

Kasai

LUNDA 15th cent.

LWENA

LOZI 19th cent.

LUCHAZI

MBUNDA

Zambezi

Cuando

TEKE fl. 15th cent.

LOANGO

KAKONGO fl. 15th cent.

NGOYO fl. 15th cent.

KONGO fl. 15th cent.

Zaïre

Loango 1650
Cabinda 1700

Mpinda 1500
São Salvador

JAGA 16th cent.

NDONGO fl. 15th cent.

MBUNDU fl. 15th cent.

MBANGALA 17th cent.

Kassange 1650

St Paul de Loanda 1600

Cuanza

CHOKWE 16th cent.

OVIMBUNDU fl. 15th cent.

Benguela 1700

Mocamedes 1825

Cunene

JAGA 16th cent.   Kingdom and date of foundation where known

→ Principal trade route

↑ Approximate date when town became important commercial centre
1500

0 100 200 300 miles
0 200 400 km

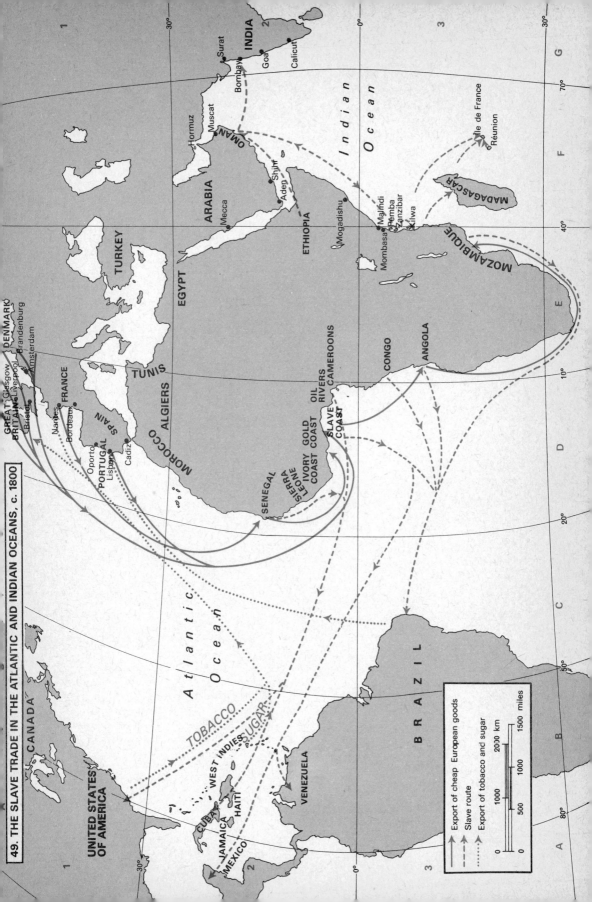

49. THE SLAVE TRADE IN THE ATLANTIC AND INDIAN OCEANS, c. 1800

Export of cheap European goods
Slave route
Export of tobacco and sugar

Scale:
0 500 1000 1500 miles
0 1000 2000 km

CANADA

UNITED STATES OF AMERICA

MEXICO

JAMAICA
HAITI
CUBA
WEST INDIES
SUGAR

VENEZUELA

BRAZIL

Atlantic Ocean

TOBACCO

GREAT BRITAIN
Glasgow
Liverpool
Bristol
DENMARK
Brandenburg
Amsterdam
Nantes
Bordeaux
FRANCE
SPAIN
Oporto
Lisbon
PORTUGAL
Cadiz

TUNIS
ALGIERS
MOROCCO
TURKEY

EGYPT

ARABIA
Mecca
Aden
Shihr
Muscat
Hormuz
OMAN

ETHIOPIA

SENEGAL
SIERRA LEONE
IVORY COAST
GOLD COAST
SLAVE COAST
OIL RIVERS
CAMEROONS

CONGO

ANGOLA

MOZAMBIQUE

Mogadishu
Malindi
Mombasa
Pemba
Zanzibar
Kilwa

MADAGASCAR

Île de France
Réunion

INDIA
Surat
Bombay
Goa
Calicut

Indian Ocean

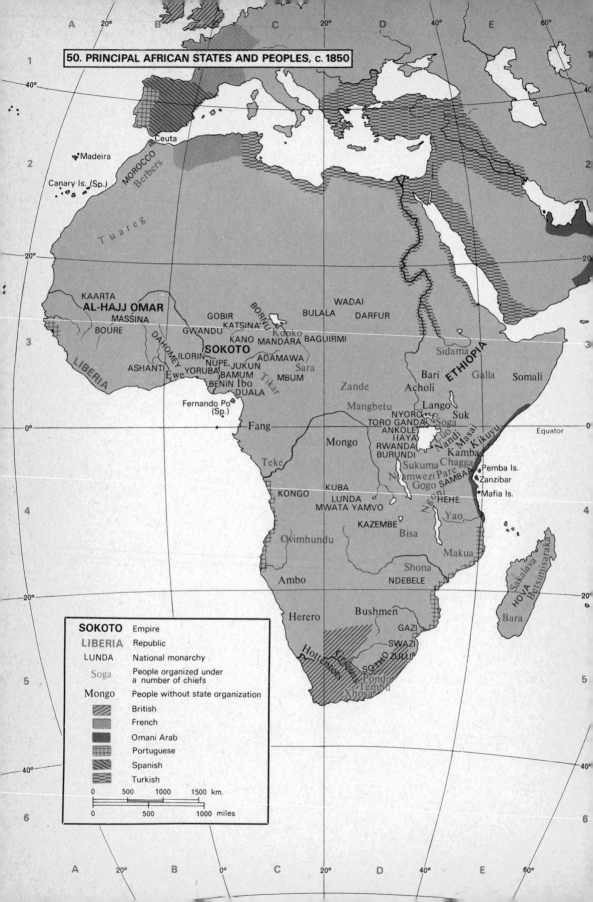

50. PRINCIPAL AFRICAN STATES AND PEOPLES, c. 1850

Ceuta
Madeira
Canary Is. (Sp.)

MOROCCO
Berbers

Tuareg

KAARTA
AL-HAJJ OMAR
MASSINA
BOURE
GOBIR
KATSINA
GWANDU
BORNU
Kooko
WADAI
BULALA
DARFUR
LIBERIA
DAHOMEY
ILORIN
SOKOTO
KANO MANDARA BAGUIRMI
ASHANTI
NUPE JUKUN
ADAMAWA
Sidama
ETHIOPIA
Ewe YORUBA BAMUM
Sara
Bari
Galla
Somali
BENIN Ibo
MBUM
Zande
Acholi
DUALA
Tikar
Mangbetu
Lango
Fernando Po
(Sp.)
NYORO
Suk
TORO GANDA
Soga
Fang
Luo
Masai
Kikuyu
ANKOLE
Nandi
Mongo
HAYA
Kamba
RWANDA
Chagga
Pemba Is.
Teke
BURUNDI
Pare
Zanzibar
Sukuma
SAMBA
Nyamwezi
Mafia Is.
KUBA
Gogo
KONGO
LUNDA
Ngoni
HEHE
MWATA YAMVO
Yao
KAZEMBE
Bisa
Ovimbundu
Makua
Ambo
Shona
Sakalava
NDEBELE
HOVA
Betsimisaraka
Herero
Bushmen
Bara
GAZI
SWAZI
Hottentots
Griqua
ZULU
SOTHO
Pondo
Tembu
Xhosa

Equator

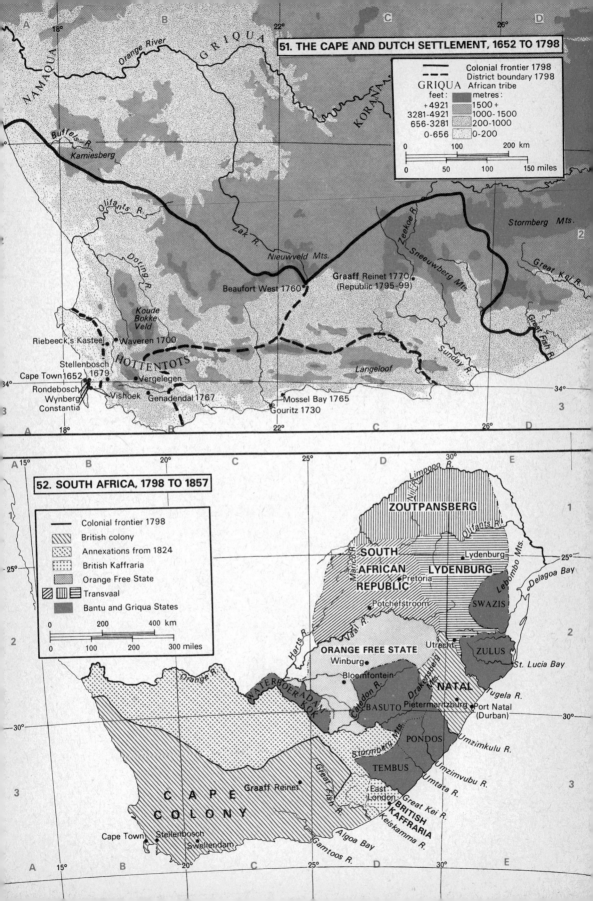

51. THE CAPE AND DUTCH SETTLEMENT, 1652 TO 1798

Colonial frontier 1798
District boundary 1798
African tribe

GRIQUA

feet:
+4921
3281-4921
656-3281
0-656

metres:
1500 +
1000-1500
200-1000
0-200

0   100   200 km
0   50   100   150 miles

NAMAQUA

Orange River

GRIQUA

KORANA

Buffels R.
Kamiesberg

Olifants R.

Doring R.

Zak R.

Nieuwveld Mts.

Stormberg Mts.

Zeekoe R.
Sneeuwberg Mts.

Great Kei R.

Beaufort West 1760
Graaff Reinet 1770
(Republic 1795-99)

Koude Bokke Veld

Riebeeck's Kasteel   Waveren 1700
Stellenbosch 1679
Cape Town 1652
Rondebosch
Wynberg
Constantia

HOTTENTOTS

Vergelegen
Vishoek   Genadendal 1767
Gouritz 1730
Mossel Bay 1765

Langeloof

Sunday R.

Great Fish R.

52. SOUTH AFRICA, 1798 TO 1857

Colonial frontier 1798
British colony
Annexations from 1824
British Kaffraria
Orange Free State
Transvaal
Bantu and Griqua States

0   200   400 km
0   100   200   300 miles

ZOUTPANSBERG

Limpopo R.

SOUTH AFRICAN REPUBLIC

Marico R.

Olifants R.

LYDENBURG

Lydenburg

Pretoria

Lebombo Mts.

Delagoa Bay

Potchefstroom

Vaal R.

SWAZIS

ORANGE FREE STATE

Harts R.

Winburg

Utrecht

ZULUS

St. Lucia Bay

WATERBOER ADAM KOK

Orange R.

Bloemfontein

Caledon R.

BASUTO

Drakensberg Mts.

NATAL

Pietermaritzburg

Port Natal (Durban)

Tugela R.

Umzimkulu R.

PONDOS

Stormberg Mts.

TEMBUS

Great Fish R.

Umzimvubu R.

Umtata R.

C A P E
C O L O N Y

Graaff Reinet

East London

BRITISH KAFFRARIA

Great Kei R.
Keiskamma R.

Cape Town
Stellenbosch
Swellendam

Algoa Bay

Gamtoos R.

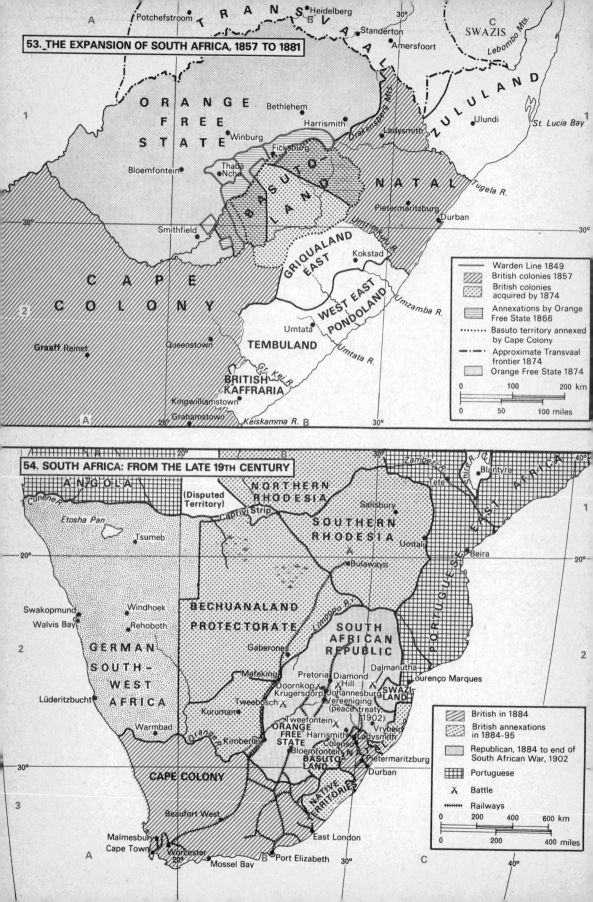

53. THE EXPANSION OF SOUTH AFRICA, 1857 TO 1881

TRANS-
Potchefstroom
Heidelberg
Standerton
Amersfoort
SWAZIS
Lebombo Mts.

ORANGE
FREE
STATE
Bethlehem
Harrismith
ZULULAND
Ulundi
St. Lucia Bay

Winburg
Ficksburg
Drakensberg Mts.
Ladysmith

BASUTO-
LAND
Thaba
Nchu
Bloemfontein

NATAL
Tugela R.

Smithfield

Umzimkulu R.
Pietermaritzburg
Durban

GRIQUALAND
EAST
Kokstad

CAPE
COLONY

WEST EAST
PONDOLAND
Umzamba R.

Graaff Reinet

Queenstown
Umtata
TEMBULAND
Umtata R.

BRITISH
KAFFRARIA
Gr. Kei R.

Kingwilliamstown
Grahamstown
Keiskamma R.

—	Warden Line 1849
▨	British colonies 1857
▨	British colonies acquired by 1874
▤	Annexations by Orange Free State 1866
····	Basuto territory annexed by Cape Colony
—·—	Approximate Transvaal frontier 1874
▨	Orange Free State 1874

0   100   200 km
0   50   100 miles

54. SOUTH AFRICA: FROM THE LATE 19TH CENTURY

ANGOLA
(Disputed Territory)
Caprivi Strip
NORTHERN RHODESIA
Zambezi R.
Tete
Blantyre
Cunene R.
Etosha Pan
SOUTHERN RHODESIA
Salisbury
Tsumeb
Uontali
Beira
Bulawaya

BECHUANALAND
PROTECTORATE
Limpopo R.

Swakopmund
Windhoek
Rehoboth
GERMAN
SOUTH-
WEST
AFRICA
Gaberones
SOUTH
AFRICAN
REPUBLIC

Walvis Bay

Mafeking
Pretoria
Diamond
Hill
Dalmanutha
Lourenço Marques

Lüderitzbucht
Doornkop
Krugersdorp
Johannesburg
SWAZI-
LAND
Kuruman
Tweebosch
Vereeniging
(peace treaty)
(1902)
Vryheid
Warmbad
Tweefontein
ORANGE
FREE
STATE
Harrismith
Ladysmith
Kimberley
Colenso
NATAL
Bloemfontein
Pietermaritzburg
BASUTO-
LAND
Durban

CAPE COLONY
NATIVE
TERRITORIES

Beaufort West

Malmesbury
Cape Town
Worcester
Mossel Bay
East London
Port Elizabeth

▨	British in 1884
▨	British annexations in 1884-95
▥	Republican, 1884 to end of South African War, 1902
▦	Portuguese
X	Battle
++++	Railways

0   200   400   600 km
0   200   400 miles

PORTUGUESE EAST AFRICA

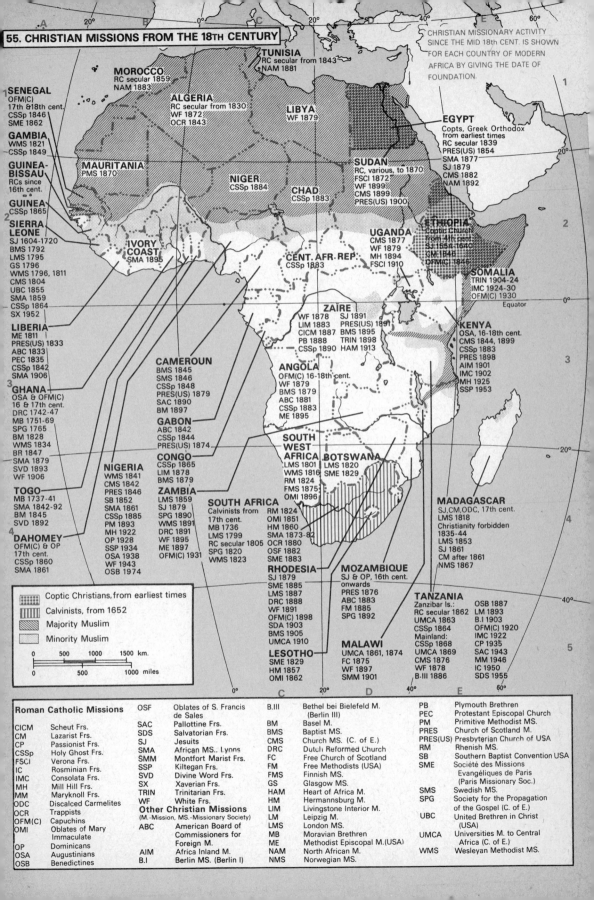

55. CHRISTIAN MISSIONS FROM THE 18TH CENTURY

CHRISTIAN MISSIONARY ACTIVITY SINCE THE MID 18TH CENT. IS SHOWN FOR EACH COUNTRY OF MODERN AFRICA BY GIVING THE DATE OF FOUNDATION.

SENEGAL
OFM(C)
17th & 18th cent.
CSSp 1846
SME 1862

GAMBIA
WMS 1821
CSSp 1849

GUINEA-BISSAU
RCs since
16th cent.

GUINEA
CSSp 1865

SIERRA LEONE
SJ 1604-1720
BMS 1792
LMS 1795
GS 1796
WMS 1796, 1811
CMS 1804
UBC 1855
SMA 1859
CSSp 1864
SX 1952

LIBERIA
ME 1811
PRES(US) 1833
ABC 1833
PEC 1835
CSSp 1842
SMA 1906

GHANA
OSA & OFM(C)
16 & 17th cent.
DRC 1742-47
MB 1751-69
SPG 1765
BM 1828
WMS 1834
BR 1847
SMA 1879
SVD 1893
WF 1906

TOGO
MB 1737-41
SMA 1842-92
BM 1845
SVD 1892

DAHOMEY
OFM(C) & OP
17th cent.
CSSp 1860
SMA 1861

MOROCCO
RC secular 1859
NAM 1883

ALGERIA
RC secular from 1830
WF 1872
OCR 1843

MAURITANIA
PMS 1870

IVORY COAST
SMA 1895

NIGER
CSSp 1884

TUNISIA
RC secular from 1843
NAM 1881

LIBYA
WF 1879

CHAD
CSSp 1883

CENT. AFR. REP.
CSSp 1883

CAMEROUN
BMS 1845
SMS 1846
CSSp 1848
PRES(US) 1879
SAC 1890
BM 1897

GABON
ABC 1842
CSSp 1844
PRES(US) 1874

CONGO
CSSp 1865
LIM 1878
BMS 1879

NIGERIA
WMS 1841
CMS 1842
PRES 1846
SB 1852
SMA 1861
CSSp 1885
PM 1893
MH 1922
OP 1928
SSP 1934
OSA 1938
WF 1943
OSB 1974

ZAMBIA
LMS 1859
SJ 1879
SPG 1890
WMS 1891
DRC 1891
WF 1895
ME 1899
OFM(C) 1931

SOUTH AFRICA
Calvinists from
17th cent.   RM 1824
MB 1736   OMI 1851
LMS 1799   HM 1860
RC secular 1805 SMA 1873-82
SPG 1820   OCR 1880
WMS 1823   OSF 1882
              SME 1883

RHODESIA
SJ 1879
SME 1885
LMS 1887
DRC 1888
WF 1891
OFM(C) 1898
SDA 1903
BMS 1905
UMCA 1910

LESOTHO
SME 1829
HM 1857
OMI 1862

EGYPT
Copts, Greek Orthodox
from earliest times
RC secular 1839
PRES(US) 1854
SMA 1877
SJ 1879
CMS 1882
NAM 1892

SUDAN
RC, various, to 1870
FSCI 1872
WF 1899
CMS 1899
PRES(US) 1900

ETHIOPIA
Coptic Church
from 4th cent.
SJ 1555-1640
GM 1846
OFM(C) 1846

UGANDA
CMS 1877
WF 1879
MH 1894
FSCI 1910

SOMALIA
TRIN 1904-24
IMC 1924-30
OFM(C) 1930

ZAIRE
WF 1878   SJ 1891
LIM 1883   PRES(US) 1891
CICM 1887   BMS 1895
PB 1888   TRIN 1898
CSSp 1890   HAM 1913

KENYA
OSA, 16-18th cent.
CMS 1844, 1899
CSSp 1883
PRES 1898
AIM 1901
IMC 1902
MH 1925
SSP 1953

ANGOLA
OFM(C) 16-18th cent.
WF 1879
BMS 1879
ABC 1881
CSSp 1883
ME 1895

SOUTH WEST AFRICA
LMS 1801
WMS 1816
RM 1824
FMS 1875
OMI 1896

BOTSWANA
LMS 1820
SME 1829

MOZAMBIQUE
SJ & OP, 16th cent.
onwards
PRES 1876
ABC 1883
FM 1885
SPG 1892

MALAWI
UMCA 1861, 1874
FC 1875
WF 1897
SMM 1901

MADAGASCAR
SJ, CM, ODC, 17th cent.
LMS 1818
Christianity forbidden
1835-44
LMS 1853
SJ 1861
CM after 1861
NMS 1867

TANZANIA
Zanzibar Is.:   OSB 1887
RC secular 1862   LM 1893
UMCA 1863   B.I 1903
CSSp 1864   OFM(C) 1920
Mainland: IMC 1922
CSSp 1868   CP 1935
UMCA 1869   SAC 1943
CMS 1876   MM 1946
WF 1878   IC 1950
B.III 1886   SDS 1955

Legend

▦	Coptic Christians, from earliest times
▥	Calvinists, from 1652
▨	Majority Muslim
▒	Minority Muslim

Scale: 0 — 500 — 1000 — 1500 km.
0 — 500 — 1000 miles

Roman Catholic Missions

CICM	Scheut Frs.
CM	Lazarist Frs.
CP	Passionist Frs.
CSSp	Holy Ghost Frs.
FSCI	Verona Frs.
IC	Rosminian Frs.
IMC	Consolata Frs.
MH	Mill Hill Frs.
MM	Maryknoll Frs.
ODC	Discalced Carmelites
OCR	Trappists
OFM(C)	Capuchins
OMI	Oblates of Mary Immaculate
OP	Dominicans
OSA	Augustinians
OSB	Benedictines
OSF	Oblates of S. Francis de Sales
SAC	Pallottine Frs.
SDS	Salvatorian Frs.
SJ	Jesuits
SMA	African MS., Lyons
SMM	Montfort Marist Frs.
SSP	Kiltegan Frs.
SVD	Divine Word Frs.
SX	Xaverian Frs.
TRIN	Trinitarian Frs.
WF	White Frs.

Other Christian Missions
(M.-Mission, MS.-Missionary Society)

ABC	American Board of Commissioners for Foreign M.
AIM	Africa Inland M.
B.I	Berlin MS. (Berlin I)
B.III	Bethel bei Bielefeld M. (Berlin III)
BM	Basel M.
BMS	Baptist MS.
CMS	Church MS. (C. of E.)
DRC	Dutch Reformed Church
FC	Free Church of Scotland
FM	Free Methodists (USA)
FMS	Finnish MS.
GS	Glasgow MS.
HAM	Heart of Africa M.
HM	Hermannsburg M.
LIM	Livingstone Interior M.
LM	Leipzig M.
LMS	London MS.
MB	Moravian Brethren
ME	Methodist Episcopal M. (USA)
NAM	North African M.
NMS	Norwegian MS.
PB	Plymouth Brethren
PEC	Protestant Episcopal Church
PM	Primitive Methodist MS.
PRES	Church of Scotland M.
PRES(US)	Presbyterian Church of USA
RM	Rhenish M.
SB	Southern Baptist Convention USA
SME	Société des Missions Evangéliques de Paris (Paris Missionary Soc.)
SMS	Swedish M.
SPG	Society for the Propagation of the Gospel (C. of E.)
UBC	United Brethren in Christ (USA)
UMCA	Universities M. to Central Africa (C. of E.)
WMS	Wesleyan Methodist MS.

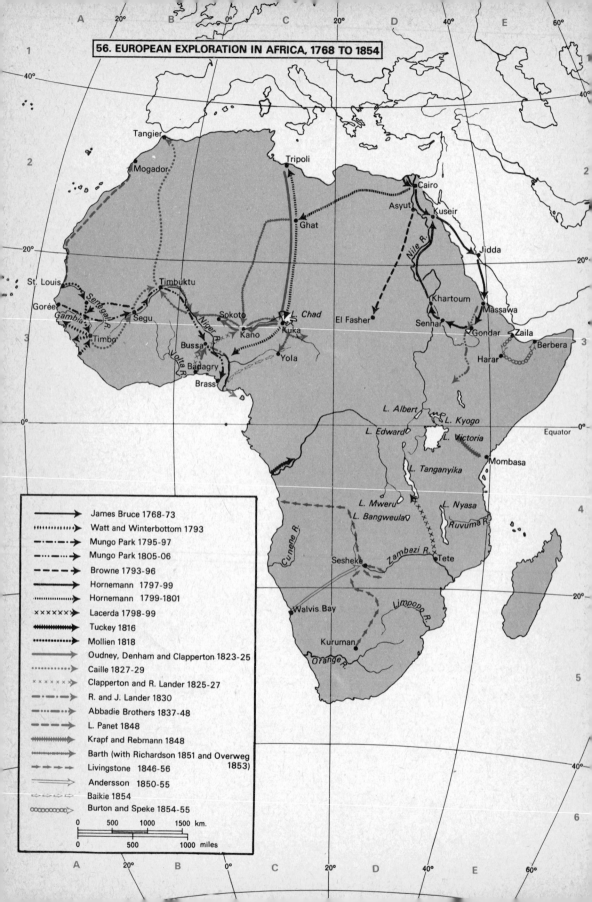

56. EUROPEAN EXPLORATION IN AFRICA, 1768 TO 1854

Tangier

Mogador

Tripoli

St. Louis

Gorée

Gambia

Senegal R.

Timbo

Segu

Timbuktu

Sokoto

Kano

Niger R.

Bussa

Volta R.

Badagry

Brass

Yola

L. Chad

Kuka

Ghat

El Fasher

Cairo

Asyut

Kuseir

Jidda

Khartoum

Massawa

Senhar

Gondar

Zaila

Berbera

Harar

Nile R.

L. Albert

L. Edward

L. Kyogo

L. Victoria

Equator

L. Tanganyika

Mombasa

L. Mweru

L. Bangweula

L. Nyasa

Ruvuma R.

Cunene R.

Sesheke

Zambezi R.

Tete

Walvis Bay

Limpopo R.

Kuruman

Orange R.

———▶	James Bruce 1768-73
···········▶	Watt and Winterbottom 1793
—·—·—▶	Mungo Park 1795-97
– – –▶	Mungo Park 1805-06
- - - -▶	Browne 1793-96
━━━━▶	Hornemann 1797-99
··········▶	Hornemann 1799-1801
×××××▶	Lacerda 1798-99
▮▮▮▮▮▶	Tuckey 1816
••••••▶	Mollien 1818
━━━━▶	Oudney, Denham and Clapperton 1823-25
·········▶	Caille 1827-29
×××××▶	Clapperton and R. Lander 1825-27
–·–·–▶	R. and J. Lander 1830
–··–··▶	Abbadie Brothers 1837-48
– – –▶	L. Panet 1848
▮▮▮▮▮▶	Krapf and Rebmann 1848
••••••▶	Barth (with Richardson 1851 and Overweg 1853)
– – –▶	Livingstone 1846-56
⇒⇒⇒▶	Andersson 1850-55
∞∞∞▶	Baikie 1854
ooooo▶	Burton and Speke 1854-55

0   500   1000   1500 km.

0   500   1000 miles

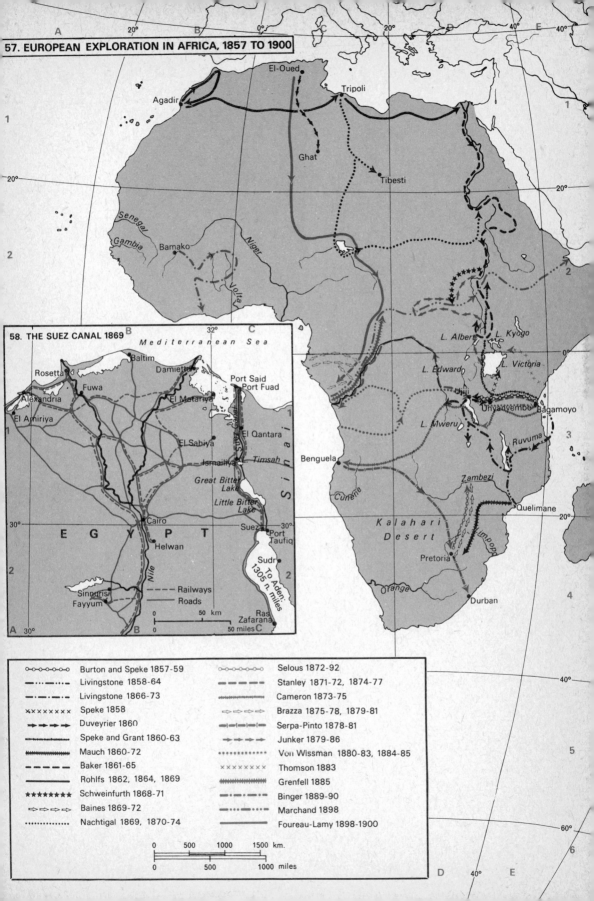

57. EUROPEAN EXPLORATION IN AFRICA, 1857 TO 1900

58. THE SUEZ CANAL 1869

Mediterranean Sea

Baltim
Rosetta
Damietta
Fuwa
Alexandria
El Matariya
Port Said
Port Fuad
El Amiriya
El Sabiya
El Qantara
Ismailiya
L. Timsah
Great Bitter Lake
Little Bitter Lake
Cairo
Suez
Port Taufiq
Helwan
E G Y P T
Sinai
Nile
Sudr
Sinnuris
Fayyum
Ras Zafarana
To Aden: 1305 n. miles

--- Railways
— Roads

0   50 km
0   50 miles

Mediterranean Sea

El-Oued
Agadir
Tripoli
Ghat
Tibesti
Senegal
Gambia
Bamako
Niger
Volta
L. Albert
L. Kyogo
L. Edward
L. Victoria
Ujiji
Unyanyembe
Bagamoyo
L. Mweru
Ruvuma
Benguela
Zambezi
Cunene
Quelimane
Kalahari Desert
Impopo
Pretoria
Orange
Durban

Legend

Burton and Speke 1857-59	Selous 1872-92
Livingstone 1858-64	Stanley 1871-72, 1874-77
Livingstone 1866-73	Cameron 1873-75
Speke 1858	Brazza 1875-78, 1879-81
Duveyrier 1860	Serpa-Pinto 1878-81
Speke and Grant 1860-63	Junker 1879-86
Mauch 1860-72	Von Wissman 1880-83, 1884-85
Baker 1861-65	Thomson 1883
Rohlfs 1862, 1864, 1869	Grenfell 1885
Schweinfurth 1868-71	Binger 1889-90
Baines 1869-72	Marchand 1898
Nachtigal 1869, 1870-74	Foureau-Lamy 1898-1900

0   500   1000   1500 km.

0   500   1000 miles

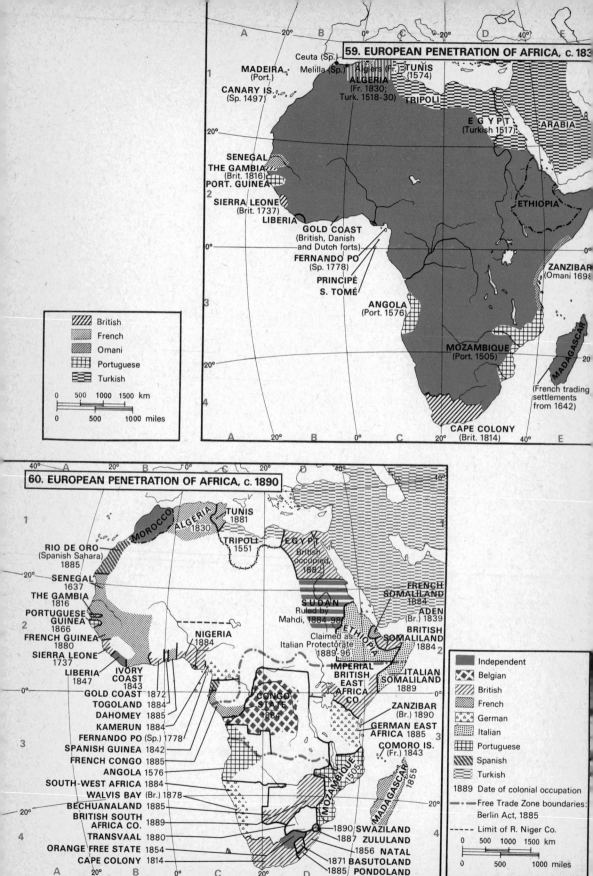

59. EUROPEAN PENETRATION OF AFRICA, c. 183[0]

Ceuta (Sp.)
Melilla (Sp.)
MADEIRA (Port.)
CANARY IS. (Sp. 1497)
Algiers (Fr.) TUNIS (1574)
ALGERIA (Fr. 1830; Turk. 1518-30)
TRIPOLI
EGYPT (Turkish 1517)
ARABIA
SENEGAL
THE GAMBIA (Brit. 1816)
PORT. GUINEA
SIERRA LEONE (Brit. 1737)
LIBERIA
GOLD COAST (British, Danish and Dutch forts)
FERNANDO PO (Sp. 1778)
PRINCIPÉ
S. TOMÉ
ANGOLA (Port. 1576)
ETHIOPIA
ZANZIBAR (Omani 1698)
MOZAMBIQUE (Port. 1505)
MADAGASCAR
(French trading settlements from 1642)
CAPE COLONY (Brit. 1814)

Legend:
- British
- French
- Omani
- Portuguese
- Turkish

0 500 1000 1500 km
0 500 1000 miles

60. EUROPEAN PENETRATION OF AFRICA, c. 1890

MOROCCO
ALGERIA 1830
TUNIS 1881
TRIPOLI 1551
EGYPT British occupied 1882
RIO DE ORO (Spanish Sahara) 1885
SENEGAL 1637
THE GAMBIA 1816
PORTUGUESE GUINEA 1866
FRENCH GUINEA 1880
SIERRA LEONE 1737
LIBERIA 1847
IVORY COAST 1843
GOLD COAST 1872
TOGOLAND 1884
DAHOMEY 1885
KAMERUN 1884
FERNANDO PO (Sp.) 1778
SPANISH GUINEA 1842
FRENCH CONGO 1885
ANGOLA 1576
SOUTH-WEST AFRICA 1884
WALVIS BAY (Br.) 1878
BECHUANALAND 1885
BRITISH SOUTH AFRICA CO. 1889
TRANSVAAL 1880
ORANGE FREE STATE 1854
CAPE COLONY 1814
NIGERIA 1884
SUDAN Ruled by Mahdi, 1884-98
FRENCH SOMALILAND 1884
ADEN (Br.) 1839
BRITISH SOMALILAND 1884
ETHIOPIA Claimed as Italian Protectorate 1889-96
IMPERIAL BRITISH EAST AFRICA CO.
ITALIAN SOMALILAND 1889
CONGO STATE 1884
ZANZIBAR (Br.) 1890
GERMAN EAST AFRICA 1885
COMORO IS. (Fr.) 1843
MOZAMBIQUE 1505
MADAGASCAR 1855
1890 SWAZILAND
1887 ZULULAND
1856 NATAL
1871 BASUTOLAND
1885 PONDOLAND

Legend:
- Independent
- Belgian
- British
- French
- German
- Italian
- Portuguese
- Spanish
- Turkish
- 1889 Date of colonial occupation
- Free Trade Zone boundaries: Berlin Act, 1885
- Limit of R. Niger Co.

0 500 1000 1500 km
0 500 1000 miles

61. PRINCIPAL AFRICAN RESISTANCE TO EUROPEAN COLONIAL PENETRATION

MOROCCO
Bilad as-Siba 1912-25
Abd al-Krim against
France and Spain
1921-26

TUNISIA
Disturbances
1952

ALGERIA
Abd al-Kadir 1834-47
Kabylia to 1857
Morani Rebellion 1871
S. Oran (Ouled Sidi
Sheikh) 1864
Rebellion against
French 1954-62

LIBYA
Resistance to
Italians 1912-31

EGYPT
Arabi Pasha
1881-82
Revolt 1919-20
Canal Zone
1954-56

Trarza resistance 1855
Ahmadou Samory 1881-98
Ahmadou 1881-93
Mahmadou Lamine
1881-87

SENEGAL

**PORT.
GUINEA**
Guerilla war
from 1963

CHAD
Rabah 1899-1900

SUDAN
Ruled by Mahdi
1884-98

Resistance against
Italy 1894-96
Battle of Adowa 1896
Guerilla Resistance to Italy
1935-41

Sayyid Muhammad
Abdille Hasan
1891-1920

GHANA

DAHOMEY

NIGERIA

ETHIOPIA

**SIERRA
LEONE**
Temne Revolt
1898-1900

CAMEROUN

Bunyoro Resistance
1890-98

UGANDA

KENYA

SOMALIA

Mbaruk bin Rashid
against Zanzibar 1882
Witu rising against
Germans 1890-93
'Mau Mau' Rising against
British 1952-55

Ashanti War 1874
Resistance 1896-1900

Gléglé 1887-89
Béhanzin 1889-94

ZAÏRE
Arab resistance
1891-94
Léopoldville
Riots 1959

TANZANIA
Abushiri rebellion against
Germans 1888-89
Hehe War 1888-98
Rebellion 1894
Machemba's Rebellion 1895
Maji-Maji Rebellion
1905-06

ZANZIBAR Rising against
British 1896

COMORO IS.
Resistance
1896-97, 1899

Fulani resistance 1890's
Itsekiri War 1893-4
Benin 1897

Resistance to Germans
Yaoundé 1896
Boulou and Bassa
1898-1901

ANGOLA

MALAWI

Arab resistance
to British –
Karonga 1891
Chilembwe's
Rising 1915

MADAGASCAR

Bakongo Rising 1913
Ovimbundu Rising 1913
Revolt against
Portuguese
from 1961

**SOUTH
WEST
AFRICA**

RHODESIA
Mashona Revolt 1896
Matabele Revolt 1896

MOZAMBIQUE
Risings 1895-99
Guerilla war against
Portuguese from 1963

Hottentot Revolt
1894, 1904-6
Herero Rebellion 1904
Nama (Bondelswart)
Revolt 1922

Resistance to French 1885-1905
Rebellion against French 1947-48

**SOUTH
AFRICA**

Zulu war 1   1879,
Zulu war 2   1893-96
Zulu Revolt 1906

- - - Modern international boundaries

0   500   1000   1500 km

0   500   1000 miles

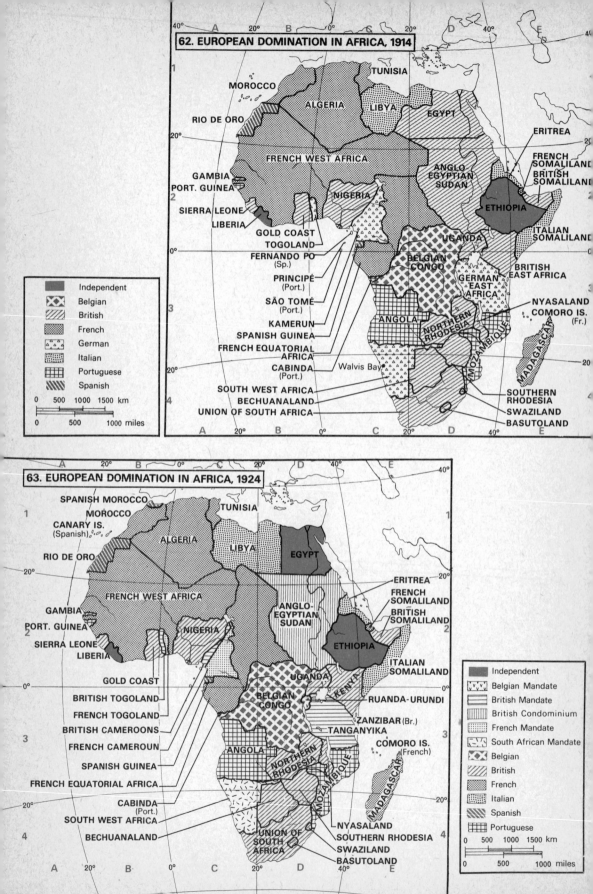

62. EUROPEAN DOMINATION IN AFRICA, 1914

MOROCCO
TUNISIA
ALGERIA
LIBYA
EGYPT
RIO DE ORO
FRENCH WEST AFRICA
ERITREA
FRENCH SOMALILAND
BRITISH SOMALILAND
GAMBIA
PORT. GUINEA
NIGERIA
ANGLO EGYPTIAN SUDAN
SIERRA LEONE
LIBERIA
ETHIOPIA
GOLD COAST
TOGOLAND
FERNANDO PO (Sp.)
UGANDA
ITALIAN SOMALILAND
PRINCIPÉ (Port.)
BELGIAN CONGO
SÃO TOMÉ (Port.)
GERMAN EAST AFRICA
BRITISH EAST AFRICA
KAMERUN
SPANISH GUINEA
ANGOLA
NYASALAND
COMORO IS. (Fr.)
FRENCH EQUATORIAL AFRICA
NORTHERN RHODESIA
CABINDA (Port.)
Walvis Bay
MOZAMBIQUE
MADAGASCAR
SOUTH WEST AFRICA
BECHUANALAND
SOUTHERN RHODESIA
UNION OF SOUTH AFRICA
SWAZILAND
BASUTOLAND

Independent
Belgian
British
French
German
Italian
Portuguese
Spanish

0 500 1000 1500 km
0 500 1000 miles

63. EUROPEAN DOMINATION IN AFRICA, 1924

SPANISH MOROCCO
MOROCCO
TUNISIA
CANARY IS. (Spanish)
ALGERIA
LIBYA
EGYPT
RIO DE ORO
FRENCH WEST AFRICA
ERITREA
FRENCH SOMALILAND
BRITISH SOMALILAND
GAMBIA
PORT. GUINEA
NIGERIA
ANGLO-EGYPTIAN SUDAN
SIERRA LEONE
LIBERIA
ETHIOPIA
GOLD COAST
ITALIAN SOMALILAND
BRITISH TOGOLAND
UGANDA
FRENCH TOGOLAND
RUANDA-URUNDI
BRITISH CAMEROONS
BELGIAN CONGO
KENYA
FRENCH CAMEROUN
ZANZIBAR (Br.)
TANGANYIKA
SPANISH GUINEA
ANGOLA
COMORO IS. (French)
FRENCH EQUATORIAL AFRICA
NORTHERN RHODESIA
CABINDA (Port.)
MOZAMBIQUE
MADAGASCAR
SOUTH WEST AFRICA
BECHUANALAND
UNION OF SOUTH AFRICA
NYASALAND
SOUTHERN RHODESIA
SWAZILAND
BASUTOLAND

Independent
Belgian Mandate
British Mandate
British Condominium
French Mandate
South African Mandate
Belgian
British
French
Italian
Spanish
Portuguese

0 500 1000 1500 km
0 500 1000 miles

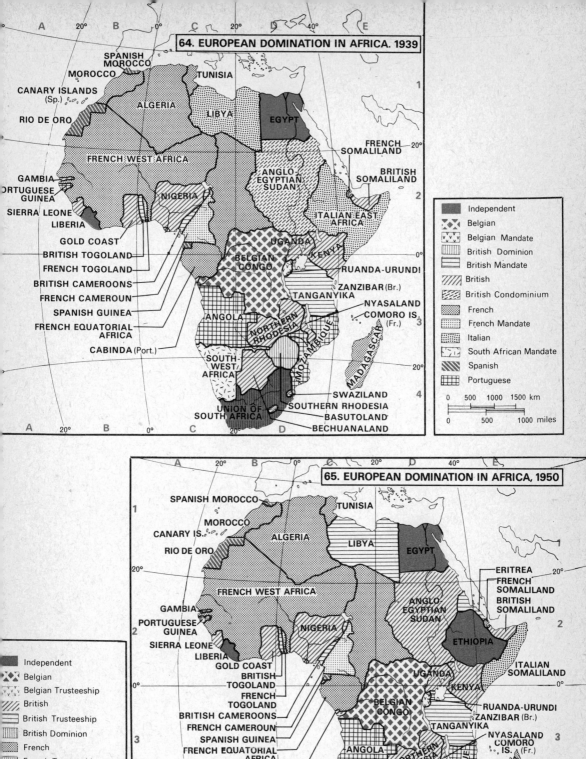

64. EUROPEAN DOMINATION IN AFRICA. 1939

SPANISH MOROCCO
MOROCCO
CANARY ISLANDS (Sp.)
RIO DE ORO
ALGERIA
TUNISIA
LIBYA
EGYPT
FRENCH SOMALILAND
FRENCH WEST AFRICA
ANGLO-EGYPTIAN SUDAN
BRITISH SOMALILAND
GAMBIA
PORTUGUESE GUINEA
NIGERIA
ITALIAN EAST AFRICA
SIERRA LEONE
LIBERIA
GOLD COAST
BRITISH TOGOLAND
FRENCH TOGOLAND
BRITISH CAMEROONS
FRENCH CAMEROUN
SPANISH GUINEA
FRENCH EQUATORIAL AFRICA
CABINDA (Port.)
UGANDA
BELGIAN CONGO
KENYA
RUANDA-URUNDI
ZANZIBAR (Br.)
TANGANYIKA
NYASALAND
COMORO IS. (Fr.)
ANGOLA
NORTHERN RHODESIA
MOZAMBIQUE
MADAGASCAR
SOUTH WEST AFRICA
SWAZILAND
SOUTHERN RHODESIA
UNION OF SOUTH AFRICA
BASUTOLAND
BECHUANALAND

Independent
Belgian
Belgian Mandate
British Dominion
British Mandate
British
British Condominium
French
French Mandate
Italian
South African Mandate
Spanish
Portuguese

0 500 1000 1500 km
0   500   1000 miles

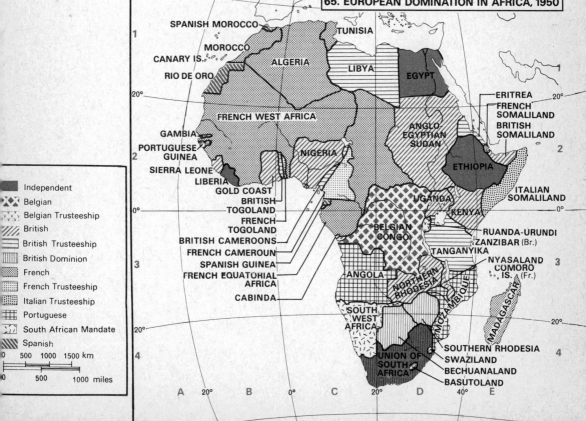

65. EUROPEAN DOMINATION IN AFRICA, 1950

SPANISH MOROCCO
MOROCCO
CANARY IS.
RIO DE ORO
ALGERIA
TUNISIA
LIBYA
EGYPT
ERITREA
FRENCH SOMALILAND
BRITISH SOMALILAND
FRENCH WEST AFRICA
ANGLO-EGYPTIAN SUDAN
GAMBIA
PORTUGUESE GUINEA
SIERRA LEONE
NIGERIA
ETHIOPIA
ITALIAN SOMALILAND
LIBERIA
GOLD COAST
BRITISH TOGOLAND
FRENCH TOGOLAND
BRITISH CAMEROONS
FRENCH CAMEROUN
SPANISH GUINEA
FRENCH EQUATORIAL AFRICA
CABINDA
UGANDA
BELGIAN CONGO
KENYA
RUANDA-URUNDI
ZANZIBAR (Br.)
TANGANYIKA
NYASALAND
COMORO IS. (Fr.)
ANGOLA
NORTHERN RHODESIA
MOZAMBIQUE
MADAGASCAR
SOUTH WEST AFRICA
SOUTHERN RHODESIA
SWAZILAND
BECHUANALAND
UNION OF SOUTH AFRICA
BASUTOLAND

Independent
Belgian
Belgian Trusteeship
British
British Trusteeship
British Dominion
French
French Trusteeship
Italian Trusteeship
Portuguese
South African Mandate
Spanish

0 500 1000 1500 km
0   500   1000 miles

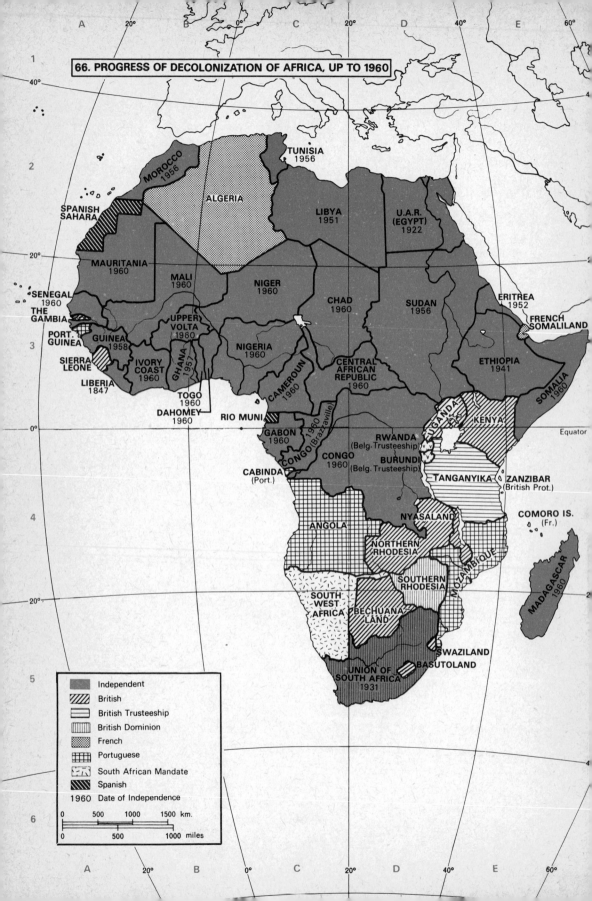

66. PROGRESS OF DECOLONIZATION OF AFRICA, UP TO 1960

MOROCCO 1956

TUNISIA 1956

ALGERIA

SPANISH SAHARA

LIBYA 1951

U.A.R. (EGYPT) 1922

MAURITANIA 1960

SENEGAL 1960

THE GAMBIA

PORT. GUINEA

GUINEA 1958

SIERRA LEONE

LIBERIA 1847

MALI 1960

UPPER VOLTA 1960

IVORY COAST 1960

GHANA 1957

TOGO 1960

DAHOMEY 1960

NIGER 1960

NIGERIA 1960

CHAD 1960

SUDAN 1956

ERITREA 1952

FRENCH SOMALILAND

ETHIOPIA 1941

SOMALIA 1960

CENTRAL AFRICAN REPUBLIC 1960

CAMEROUN 1960

RIO MUNI

GABON 1960

CONGO (Brazzaville)

CONGO 1960

RWANDA (Belg. Trusteeship)

BURUNDI (Belg. Trusteeship)

UGANDA

KENYA

CABINDA (Port.)

TANGANYIKA

ZANZIBAR (British Prot.)

Equator

COMORO IS. (Fr.)

ANGOLA

NYASALAND

NORTHERN RHODESIA

MOZAMBIQUE

MADAGASCAR 1960

SOUTHERN RHODESIA

SOUTH WEST AFRICA

BECHUANA LAND

SWAZILAND

BASUTOLAND

UNION OF SOUTH AFRICA 1931

Legend

- Independent
- British
- British Trusteeship
- British Dominion
- French
- Portuguese
- South African Mandate
- Spanish
- 1960 Date of Independence

0 500 1000 1500 km.

0 500 1000 miles

67. INDEPENDENT AFRICA, POLITICAL AND POPULATION 1975

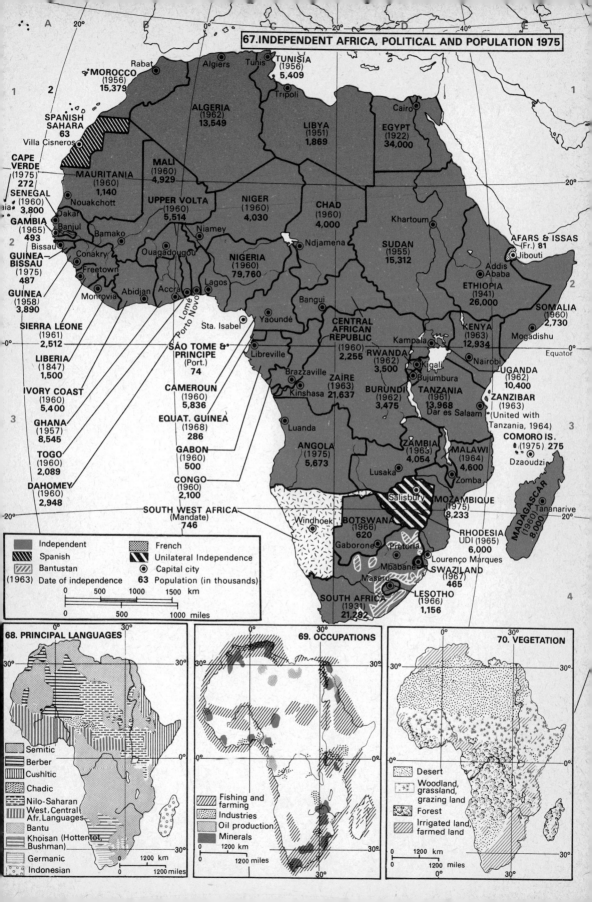

MOROCCO (1956) 15,379 — Rabat

TUNISIA (1956) 5,409 — Tunis

ALGERIA (1962) 13,549 — Algiers

LIBYA (1951) 1,869 — Tripoli

EGYPT (1922) 34,000 — Cairo

SPANISH SAHARA 63 — Villa Cisneros

CAPE VERDE (1975) 272

SENEGAL (1960) 3,800 — Dakar

GAMBIA (1965) 493 — Banjul

GUINEA-BISSAU (1975) 487 — Bissau

GUINEA (1958) 3,890 — Conakry

SIERRA LEONE (1961) 2,512 — Freetown

LIBERIA (1847) 1,500 — Monrovia

IVORY COAST (1960) 5,400 — Abidjan

GHANA (1957) 8,545 — Accra

TOGO (1960) 2,089 — Lomé

DAHOMEY (1960) 2,948 — Porto Novo

MAURITANIA (1960) 1,140 — Nouakchott

MALI (1960) 4,929 — Bamako

UPPER VOLTA (1960) 5,514 — Ouagadougou

NIGER (1960) 4,030 — Niamey

NIGERIA (1960) 79,760 — Lagos

CHAD (1960) 4,000 — Ndjamena

SUDAN (1955) 15,312 — Khartoum

CENTRAL AFRICAN REPUBLIC (1960) 2,255 — Bangui

CAMEROUN (1960) 5,836 — Yaoundé

SÃO TOMÉ & PRINCIPE (Port.) 74 — Sta. Isabel

EQUAT. GUINEA (1968) 286 — Libreville

GABON (1960) 500

CONGO (1960) 2,100 — Brazzaville

ZAIRE (1963) 21,637 — Kinshasa

RWANDA (1962) 3,500 — Kigali

BURUNDI (1962) 3,475 — Bujumbura

UGANDA (1962) 10,400 — Kampala

KENYA (1963) 12,934 — Nairobi

TANZANIA (1961) 13,968 — Dar es Salaam

ZANZIBAR (1963) (United with Tanzania, 1964)

ETHIOPIA (1941) 26,000 — Addis Ababa

AFARS & ISSAS (Fr.) 81 — Jibouti

SOMALIA (1960) 2,730 — Mogadishu

ANGOLA (1975) 5,673 — Luanda

ZAMBIA (1963) 4,054 — Lusaka

MALAWI (1964) 4,600 — Zomba

COMORO IS. (1975) 275 — Dzaoudzi

MOZAMBIQUE (1975) 8,233 — Lourenço Marques

RHODESIA UDI (1965) 6,000 — Salisbury

MADAGASCAR (1960) 8,000 — Tananarive

SOUTH WEST AFRICA (Mandate) 746 — Windhoek

BOTSWANA (1966) 620 — Gaborone

SWAZILAND (1967) 465 — Mbabane

LESOTHO (1966) 1,156 — Maseru

SOUTH AFRICA (1931) 21,282 — Pretoria

Legend

- Independent
- Spanish
- Bantustan
- (1963) Date of independence
- French
- Unilateral Independence
- ⊙ Capital city
- 63 Population (in thousands)

0   500   1000   1500 km
0   500   1000 miles

68. PRINCIPAL LANGUAGES

- Semitic
- Berber
- Cushitic
- Chadic
- Nilo-Saharan
- West, Central Afr. Languages
- Bantu
- Khoisan (Hottentot, Bushman)
- Germanic
- Indonesian

0   1200 km
0   1200 miles

69. OCCUPATIONS

- Fishing and farming
- Industries
- Oil production
- Minerals

0   1200 km
0   1200 miles

70. VEGETATION

- Desert
- Woodland, grassland, grazing land
- Forest
- Irrigated land farmed land

0   1200 km
0   1200 miles

Select Bibliography

As follows are the principal works consulted in preparing this atlas. The place of publication is mentioned only if it is outside the United Kingdom.

Ady, P.H., *Oxford Regional Economic Atlas: Africa,* 1965.

Africa Orientale Italiana, Consociazione Turistica Italiana, Milan, 1938.

Ajayi, J.F.A., and Crowder, M., *History of West Africa,* Vol.I, 1971.

Anuario Pontificio, Vatican, Rome, annually.

Arkell, A.J., *History of the Sudan from earliest times to 1821,* 1954.

Axelson, E., *South-East Africa, 1488-1530,* 1940.
 The Portuguese in South-East Africa, 1600-1700, Witwatersrand, 1960.

Barbour, N., *A Survey of North-East Africa,* 1962.

Bovill, E.W., *The Golden Trade of the Moors,* 1958.

Chapus et Dandouau, *Manuel d'Histoire de Madagascar,* Paris, 1961.

Chumovsky, T.A., *Três Roteiros Desconhecidos de Ahmad ibn Madjid,*
 trans. M. Malkiel-Jirmounsky, Lisbon, 1960.

Clark, J.D., 'The Prehistoric Origins of African Culture', *Journ. of African History,* V, 2, 1964.

Cornevin, R., *Histoire de l'Afrique,* 3 vols., Paris, 1962-1974.

Ethnographic Survey of Africa, in progress.

Fage, J.D., *An Atlas of African History,* 1963.

Filesi, T., *Le relazioni della Cina con l'Africa nel medio-evo,* Milan, 1962.

Freeman-Grenville, G.S.P., *The East African Coast: Select Documents,* 2nd edn., 1975.
 Chronology of African History, 1973.

Fox, E.W., *Atlas of American History,* New York, 1964.

Gardiner, A., *Egypt of the Pharaohs,* 1961.

Gavigan, J.J., *De vita monastica in Africa septentrionali,* Rome, 1962.

Gentil, G., *Découverte du Monde,* Paris, 1954.

Gilbert, M., *Recent History Atlas,* 1966.

Gray, J.M., *History of Zanzibar,* 1962.

Greenburg, J.H., *Studies in African Linguistic Classification,* New Haven, Connecticut, 1955.

Guides Bleus: *Afrique Occidentale Française,* Togo, Paris, 1958.
 Afrique Centrale, Paris, 1962.
 Egypte, Paris, 1956.
 Algérie, Tunisie, Paris, 1923.

Guillain, C., *Documents sur l'histoire, la géographie et le commerce de l'Afrique orientale,*
 Paris, 4 vols., 1856-1857.

Hallett, R., *Africa to 1875,* Ann Arbor, 1970.

Herodotus, *The Histories,* trans. J.E. Powell, 2 vols., 1949.

Hertslet, E., *The Map of Africa by Treaty,* 3 vols., 1909.

Hitti, P.K., *The History of the Arabs,* 7th edn., New York, 1961.

Julien, C.A., *Histoire de l'Afrique du Nord,* 2 vols., Paris, 1962.

Kamal, Prince Yusuf, *Monumenta Cartographica Africae et Aegypti,* 4 vols., Cairo, 1926-38.

Latham, N., *A Sketch-Map History of West Africa,* 1962.

Neill, S., *A History of Christian Missions,* 1964.

Oliver, R.A., 'The Problem of Bantu Expansion', *Journ. of African History,* VII, 3, 1966.

Oliver, R.A. & Mathew, A.G., *History of East Africa,* vol. I, 1963.

The Oxford Atlas.

Reyner, A.S., *Spain in Africa,* Duquesne, 1967.

Schoff, W., *The Periplus of the Erythraean Sea,* New York, 1912.
 The Periplus of Hanno, Philadelphia, 1913.

Toussaint, A., *Histoire de l'Océan Indies,* Paris, 1965.

Trimingham, J.S., *Islam in the Sudan,* 1949.
 Islam in Ethiopia, 1952.
 A History of Islam in West Africa, 1962.
 Islam in East Africa, 1964.

Ullendorf, E., *The Ethiopians,* 1965.

Walker, E.A., *Historical Atlas of South Africa,* Cape Town, 1922.
 History of Southern Africa, 1962.

Whitaker's Almanack, annually.

Index

B

Babylon, (Iraq) 12 C2, 17 D1
Babylon, (Old Cairo) 20 C2
Bacales 15 D1
Badagry 56 C3
Badajoz 30 B1
Badi 28 D3
Bagamoyo 46 B4, 57 D3
Baghdad 24 D2, 28 D2,
  29 D2, 31 D2, 32 C1
Baguirmi 43 C2, 50 C-D3
Bahariya Oasis 11 A2
El Bahnesa 11 B2
Bahr al-Ghazal, R. 43 C3
Baixos de Pracel 45 E3
Baixos de S. Antonio 45 E3
Bakongo 61 B4
Balearic Is. 14 B2, 19 B2,
  30 B1, 31 B2
Bali 33 B2
Baltim 58 B1
Baluchistan 47 C1
Bamako 57 B2, 67 B2
Bambuk 35 A1
Bamum 50 C3
Bandar Abbas 47 B2
Bangweulu, L. 46 A5,
  48 C2, 56 D4
Bangui 67 C2
Banjul 67 B2
Banu Hilal 30 B-C1
Banu Sulaim 30 B-C2
Bara 41 A-B4, 50 E5
Barawa (Brava) 28 D3,
  33 C2, 42 B2, 47 B2
Barca 24 C2, 28 C2, 29 C2,
  30 C1
Barcelona 14 B1, 17 B1,
  38 C1
Barcino (Barcelona) 14 B1
Bari 50 D3
Baroe 45 D3
Basra 28 D2, 29 D2, 47 B1
Bassa 61 B4
Basuto, Basutoland 52 D2,
  53 B1, 54 B2, 60 D4,
  62 D4, 63 D4, 64 D4,
  65 D4, 66 D5,
  and see Lesotho
Bauchi Plateau 9 C-D3,
  34 B2
Baugul 45 C-D4
Baybars 32 B1
Beaufort West 51 C2, 54 B3
Bechuanaland 54 B2, 60 D4,
  62 D4, 63 D4, 64 D4,
  65 D4, 66 D5,
  and see Botswana
Begrash (Faras) 22 B2,
  29 C2
Béhanzin 61 B4

Beira 54 C1
Beirut 32 B1
Beja 31 C3
Belgian Congo 62 D3,
  63 D3, 64 D3, 65 D3,
  and see Congo,
  and Zaïre
Bemba 48 C2
Bengal, Bay of 47 C-D2
Bengi 41 A3
Benguela 38 C4, 45 B3,
  48 A2, 57 C3
Benin 35 C2, 36 C4, 38 C3,
  40 C2, 43 B3, 44 C2,
  50 C3, 61 B4
Benin, Bight of 44 C2
Benue, R. 17 B3, 34 B2
Beraku 40 C2
Berbera 28 D3, 33 C1,
  46 C2, 47 B2, 56 E3
Berbers 50 B2
Berenice (Benghazi) 20 B1
Berenice (Egypt) 13 B1,
  22 B2
Bethlehem (S. Africa) 53 B1
Betsileo 41 B3
Betsimaraka 41 B2-3, 50 E4
Beyin 40 B2
Biafra, Bight of 40 C2,
  44 C2
Bilad as-Siba 61 B2
Bilma 17 C2, 28 B3, 29 B3,
  31 B3, 34 B2, 36 D3
Biram 43 C2, 44 C1
Bir Gao 46 C4
Bisa 48 C2, 50 D4
Biskra 24 B2
Bissagos Is. 38 B3, 40 A2
Bissau 40 B2, 67 B2
Bita 42 B2
Bithynia 17 D1
Black Sea 12 B1
Blanco, C. 38 B3, 43 A2
Blantyre 54 C1
Bloemfontein 52 D2, 53 B1,
  54 B2
Bocas de Cuamas 45 D3
Bojador, C. 38 B2, 43 A2
Bombay 47 C2, 49 G2
Bombetoc Bay 41 B2
Boina 41 B2
Bône 28 B2, 37 B2
Bonny 40 C2
Bordeaux 49 D1
Borgu 44 C1
Borku 29 C2
Bornu 35 D1, 36 D3, 43 C2,
  44 D2, 50 C3
Botswana 1 D3-4, 55 D3-4,
  67 D3-4,
  and see Bechuanaland
Bougie 30 B1, 31 B2, 36 C1
Boulou 61 B4

Boure 50 B3
Bramas 45 B2
Brandenburg 49 E1
Brass 56 C3
Brazil 49 B-C3
Brazzaville 67 C3
Bristol 49 D1
Britain 23 A1, 49 D1
British Cameroons 63 C2
  64 C2, 65 C2
British East Africa 62 D-E2-3,
  and see Kenya
British Kaffraria 52 D3,
  53 B2
British Somaliland 60 E2,
  62 E2, 63 E2, 64 E2,
  65 E2, and see Somalia
British South Africa Co.
  60 D3-4
British Togoland 63 C2,
  64 C2, 65 C2
Broken Hill 4 D3, 6 D3
Bubastis 11 B1
Buffels, R. 51 A-B1
Buganda 26 C3, 46 B3,
  50 D3
Bujumbura 67 D3
Bulala 50 C3
Bulama 40 A1
Bulawayo 54 B2
Bulla 19 B2
Bunce Is. 40 A2
Bundu 35 A1
Bunyoro 46 B3, 50 D3,
  61 D3
Burma 47 D2
Burundi 1 D3, 46 A-B4,
  50 D4, 66 D4, 67 D3,
  and see Ruanda-Urundi
Bushire 47 B2
Bushmen 7 B3, 50 D5
Busiris 11 B1
Busoga 46 B3
Busra 32 B1
Bussa 56 C3
Buto 11 B1
Butre 40 B2
Butua 48 C3
Byzacena 18 B2, 19 A2
Byzantine Empire 28 C1,
  31 C1-2

C

Cabinda 1 C3, 45 B2, 48 A2,
  62 B4, 63 B4, 64 B3,
  65 B3, 66 C4
Cabral, Pedro Alvares 38 D4
Cacheu 40 A1
Cadiz 49 D1
Caesarea (Asia Minor) 32 B1
Caesarea (Cherchel) 16 B2,
  18 B2, 19 B2

57

Rusaddir (Melilla) 14 A2,
16 A2
Rusicadae 16 B2, 18 B2,
19 B2
Rusinga Is. 4 D3
Ruvuma, R. 4 D3, 6 D4,
33 B4, 45 D3, 46 B5,
48 D2, 56 D4, 57 D3
Rwanda 1 D3, 46 A-B4,
50 D4, 66 D4, 67 D3

S

Sab 46 C3
Sabaeans 17 E2
Sabaki, R. 46 B4,
Sabi, R. 48 C3
Sabratha 19 C2
Saga 42 C1
Sagres 38 B2
Saguntum 14 A2, 17 B1
Sahadia 41 A3
El Sahiya 58 C1
Sai 13 B1
al-Saif al-Tawil 42 C2
St. Agulhas 45 B5
St. Catherine, C. 38 C4
St. Catherine's Monastery
38 D2
St. Helena Bay 38 C5
St. Helena, C. 45 B5
St. Joseph 40 A1
St. Louis 40 A1, 56 B3
St. Lucia Bay 52 E2, 53 C1
St. Paul de Loanda
see Loanda
Ste. Marie Is. 41 C2
Sakalava 41 A3, 50 E4
Sakkara 11 B2
Sala 14 A2, 16 A2
Salaga 35 B2, 36 B4
Saldae (Bougie) 14 B2,
16 B2, 18 B2
Saldanha 6 C4
Sale 30 B1, 37 A2
Salisbury (Rhodesia) 54 C1,
67 D3
Samaria 12 B2
Sambaa 50 D4
Sanaa 17 D2
Sanhaja 30 A-B2, 36 A2
Sanjagi 42 B3
Sta. Isabel 67 C2
Santa Maria 38 B3
Santa Maria, C. 38 C4
Santarem, João de 38 C3
São Bras 38 D5
São Salvador 48 A2
São Tomé 59 B3, 62 B3,
67 C3
Sara 50 C3
Saragossa 28 A1, 29 A1,
30 B1

Sardinia 19 B1-2
Sarjal Is. 42 F2
Save, R. 48 C3
Sawahil 42 B2-3
Sefar 6 C1
Segu 44 B1, 56 B3
Sekondi 40 B2
Seljuk Turks 31 C-D1-2,
32 B1
Semna 13 B1
Sena 48 C3
Senegal 1 B2, 40 A1, 49 D2,
55 A1, 59 B2, 60 B2,
61 B3, 66 B3, 67 B2
Senegal, R. 4 B2, 6 B2,
34 A2, 43 A2, 44 A1,
56 B3, 57 B2
Senill or Sunis 38 A2
Sennar 13 B2, 17 D2, 22 B3,
28 C3, 56 D3
Septem (Ceuta) 19 A2
Serapion 17 D3
Sesheke 56 D4
Setif 31 B2
Seville 30 B1, 31 A2
Seychelles Is. 47 B3
Sfax 31 B2
Shaheinab 6 D2
Shama 40 B2
Sheik 4 E2
Sherbro 40 A2
Shibeli, R. 33 C2, 46 C3
Shido 40 C2
Shihr 33 C1, 42 C1, 46 C2,
47 B2, 49 F2
Shire, R. 48 D3, 54 C1
Shoa 33 B2, 46 B3
Shona 50 D4
Shumatra 42 F2-3
Shungo-Shungaa Is. 42 B3
Shungwaya 33 C3
al-Siam 42 F2
Siam 47 D2
Sicca 16 B2, 18 B2
Sicily 14 C2, 30 C1
Sidama 50 D3
Sidi Abdurrahman 4 B1
Sidi Zin 4 C1
Sidon 12 B2, 32 B1
Sierra Leone 1 B2, 38 B3,
43 A3, 49 D2, 55 A2,
59 B2, 60 A2, 61 B3,
62 B2, 63 B2, 64 B2,
65 B2, 66 B3, 67 B2
Sijilmasa 29 A2, 30 B1,
31 A2, 36 B1, 37 A2,
43 B1
Sile 11 B1
al-Sin 42 G1
Sinai 11 B2, 58 C1
Sinda 42 G3
Singa 6 D2
Siniah 42 G1

Sinnuris 58 B2
Siraf 28 D2, 42 C1
Sis 32 B1
Sitifis (Setif) 16 B2, 18 B2,
19 B2
Siwa 12 A3, 15 D1, 28 C2
Slave Coast 40 C2, 49 D2
Smithfield 53 B2
Smyrna 28 C2
Sneeuwberg Mts. 51 C2
Soba 22 B3, 29 C3, 31 C3
Socotra 17 E2, 28 D3,
38 E3, 42 C2
Sofala 28 C4, 33 B5, 38 D5,
42 B4, 45 D3, 48 C3
Soga 50 D3
Sohag 11 B2
Sokna 36 D2
Sokoto 50 C3, 56 C3
Solwezi 6 D3
Somali 33 C2, 50 E3
Somalia 1 E2, 47 B2, 55 E2,
61 E3, 66 E3, 67 E2
Songhai 9 B-C3, 26 B3,
34 B2, 35 C1, 36 C3,
43 B2
Songo 45 D2
Songye 48 B-C1
Soninke 9 A-B3
Sosso 31 A3, 34 A2
Soterias Limen 13 B2
Sotho 50 D5
South Africa, Republic of
1 D4, 55 C-D4, 61 D5,
67 C-D4
South Africa, Union of
62 B4, 63 C-D4, 64 C-D4,
65 C-D4, 66 C-D5
South African Republic
52 D2
South Oran 61 B2
South West Africa 1 C4,
54 A2, 55 C4, 60 B3,
61 C4-5, 62 B4, 63 B4,
64 C4, 65 C4, 66 C5,
67 C4
Southern Rhodesia 54 B1,
62 E4, 63 E4, 64 D-E4,
65 D-E4, 66 D4,
and see Rhodesia
Spain 14 A2, 19 A1, 23 A1,
24 A1-2, 28 A1-2, 49 D1
Spanish Equatorial Guinea
see Equatorial Guinea
Spanish Morocco 63 A-B1,
64 B1, 65 A-B1
Spanish Sahara 1 B1, 60 B1,
62 B1, 63 B1, 64 B1, 65 B1,
66 B2, 67 B1
Springbok Flats 6 D4
Standerton 53 B1
Stellenbosch 4 D4, 51 B2,
52 B3

61

Sterkfontein 4 D4
Stormberg Mts. 51 D2, 52 D3
Suakin 32 B3, 38 D3, 47 B2
Sudan 1 D2, 42 B2, 47 A2, 55 D2, 60 D2, 61 D3, 66 D3, 67 D2, and see Anglo-Egyptian Sudan
Sudd Marshes 9 E4, 13 B3, 17 D3, 22 B4
Sudr 58 C2
Suez 38 D2, 58 C2
Suez Canal 58 C1-2
Suk 50 D3
Sukuma 46 B4, 50 D4
Sumatra 47 D2-3
Sunday, R. 51 C2
Sur 47 B2
Surat 49 G2
Susa 12 C2, 17 D1
Swakopmund 54 A2
Swartkrans 4 D4
Swazi, Swaziland 1 D4, 50 D5, 52 E2, 53 C1, 54 C2, 60 E4, 62 E4, 63 E4, 64 E4, 65 D-E4, 66 D5, 67 D4
Swellendam 52 C3
Syene 12 B3, 13 B1, 15 D1, 20 C2, 22 B2
Syracuse 15 C1
Syria 17 D1, 23 C2, 24 C2

T

Tabagat 42 C2
Tabenekka 30 B2
Tacapae 16 C2, 18 C2
Tachengit 4 C1
Tademekka 36 C2
Tademelt 37 B3
Tafareit 6 B1
Tafilalet 29 A2
Tagant 34 A2
Taghaza 43 B2
Takaze, R. 22 B3
Takedda 36 D3
Takoradi 40 B2
Takrama 40 B2
Talak 9 C3
Tamatave 41 B3, 47 B3
Tamedelt 29 A2
Tana, L. 13 B2, 22 B3, 46 B2
Tana, R. 46 B4
Tananarive 41 B3, 67 E3
Tanga 47 B3
Tangant 9 B2
Tanganyika 63 D3, 64 D3, 65 D3, 66 D4, and see Tanzania

Tanganyika, L. 45 C2, 46 A4, 48 C2, 56 D4
Tangier 30 B1, 31 A2, 37 A2, 56 B2
Tanis 11 B1, 22 B1
Tantum 40 B2
Tanzania 1 D3, 26 D4, 55 E5, 61 D4, 67 D3
Tarsus 32 B1
Tartus 32 B1
Tassili-n-Ajjer 9 C2, 17 C2
Taungs 4 D4
Taza 30 B1
Teggaza 36 B2, 37 A3
Teke 48 A-B1, 50 C4
Tekrur 31 A3, 34 A2, 35 A1, 36 A3, 43 A2
Tel el Amarna 11 B2
Temara 4 B1
Tembu, Tembuland 50 D5, 52 D3, 53 B2
Temne 61 B3
Tenere 9 D2
Tenth Milestone 19 B2
Ternifin 4 B1
Terra de S. Andrea 45 E3
Terra Sancti Raffael 45 D2
Teshe 40 C2
Tete 48 C3, 54 C1, 56 D4
Thaba Nchu 53 B1
Thagaste 16 B2, 18 B2
Thamugadi 16 B2, 18 B2
Thapsus 14 C2
Thebaid 20 C2, 22 A2
Thebes (Thebae) 9 F2, 11 B2, 12 B3, 15 D1, 20 C2, 22 B2
Theveste 14 B2, 16 B2, 18 B2
Thinis 12 B2
Thugga 14 B2, 16 B2
Thysdrus 16 C2, 18 C2
Tibesti 9 D2, 17 C2, 29 B2, 30 C2, 37 C3, 57 C1
Tiflis 32 C1
Tigre 46 B2
Tigris, R. 12 C2, 32 C1
Tihodaine 4 C1
Tikar 50 C3
Timbo 56 B3
Timbuktu 9 B3, 26 B4, 28 A3, 34 A2, 35 B1, 36 B3, 43 B2, 44 B1, 56 B3
Timsah, L. 58 C1
Tingi, Tingis (Tangier) 14 A2, 15 B1, 16 A2, 17 A1, 18 A2
Tinha 11 B2
Tinmel (Tin-Mahal) 31 A2
Tintinque 41 B2
Tipasa 15 C1, 16 B2, 18 B2
Tlemcen 28 A2, 31 A2, 37 A2

Togo 1 C2, 40 C2, 55 A4, 66 C3, 67 B3
Togoland 60 B3, 62 B2
Toledo 31 A1
Tombos 13 B2
Tordesillas, treaty 39 passim
Toro 46 A-B3, 50 D3
Transvaal 60 B4
Trarza 61 B2
Trasimene, L. 14 C1
Trebizond 32 B1
Tripoli (Lebanon) 32 B1
Tripoli (Libya) 16 C2, 18 C2, 24 B2, 28 B2, 30 C1, 31 B2, 34 B1, 36 D1, 37 C2, 56 C2, 57 C1, 59 C1, 60 C1, 67 C1
Tripolitania 18 B2, 19 A2
Tristao, Nuno 38 B3
Tsumeb 54 A1
Tuareg 50 B2
Tugela, R. 52 E2, 53 C1
Tulear 41 A4
Tunis 14 C2, 28 B2, 30 C1, 31 B2, 36 D1, 37 C2, 49 D1, 59 C1, 60 C1, 67 C1
Tunisia 1 C1, 55 C1, 61 C2, 62 C1, 63 C1, 64 C1, 65 C1, 66 C2, 67 C1
Turkey 49 E1
Turks 31 C-D1-2, 32 B1, 37 B-E2-3, 59 D-E1
Tweebosch 54 B2
Twin Rivers 6 D3
Tyre 12 B2, 15 D1, 17 D1, 32 B1

U

Uan Muhuggiag 6 C1
Uganda 1 D2, 55 D2, 61 D3, 62 D2, 63 D2, 64 D2, 65 D2, 66 D3, 67 E3
Ujiji 57 D3
Ulundi 53 C1
Umayyads 29 A1
Umtali 54 C1
Umtata 53 B2
Umtata, R. 52 D3, 53 B2
Umzamba, R. 53 C2
Umzimkulu, R. 52 E3, 53 B-C2-3
Umzimvubu, R. 52 D3
United Arab Republic (U.A.R.) see Egypt
United States of America 49 A1
Unyanyembe 46 B4, 57 D3
Upper Egypt (Thebaid) 20 C2
Upper Volta 1 B2, 66 B3, 67 B-C2
Utica 14 C2
Utrecht 52 E2

V

Vaal, R. 52 D2
Valencia 28 A2, 30 B1,
   31 A2, 38 B2
Vangue 45 C1
Velho, Gonzalho 38 A2
Venezuela 49 B2
Venice 28 B1, 29 B1
Vereeniging 54 B2
Vergelegen 51 B3
Vescera 16 B2, 18 B2
Victoria Falls 4 D3
Victoria, L. 10 C2, 33 B3,
   45 D2, 46 B4, 48 C1,
   56 D4, 57 D3
Villa Cisneros 67 B1
Vishoek 51 B3
Vohemar 41 C1
Volta, R. 4 B-C2, 6 B-C2,
   34 A2, 35 B2, 43 B3,
   56 B-C3, 57 B2
Volubilis 16 A2
Vryheid 54 C2

W

Wadai 26 C2, 36 D3,
   43 C2, 50 D3
Wadan 43 A2
Wagadugu 43 B2, 44 B1,
   and see Ouagadougou
Walata 28 A3, 35 B1,
   36 B3, 43 B2, 44 B1
Walvis Bay 38 C5, 54 A2,
   56 C5, 60 C3, 62 C4
Wami, R. 46 B4
Wamira Is. 42 B3
Wangara 34 A2
Warmbad 54 A2
Warri 40 C2

Wasini Is. 42 B3
Waterberg 6 D4
Waterboer 52 C2
Waveren 51 B2
West Indies 49 B2
West Pondoland 53 B2
Whydah 40 C2
Winburg 52 D2, 53 B1
Windhoek 54 A2, 67 C4
Winneba 40 C2
Witu 61 D-E4
Wolof 36 A3, 43 A2,
   44 A1
Worcester 54 A3
Wynberg 51 B3

X

Xhosa 50 D5
Xois 11 B1

Y

Yanbu 32 B2, 47 B2
Yao 50 D4
Yaoundé 61 B4, 67 C2
Yatenga 36 B3, 43 B2,
   44 B1
Yauri 43 B2
Yayo 4 C2
Yeha 22 B3
Yemen 22 C3, 23 D3,
   24 D3, 33 C1, 47 B2
Yobe, R. 6 C2, 9 C-D3
Yola 56 C3
Yoruba 35 C2

Z

Zaghawa 31 C3
Zaila 28 D3, 33 C1, 38 E3,
   46 C2, 47 B2, 56 E3

Zaïre 1 C3, 26 C4, 55 D3,
   61 D3, 67 D3
Zaïre, R. 4 C-D2-3,
   6 C-D2-3, 10 B-C1-2,
   45 B2
Zak, R. 51 B2
Zalacca 30 B1
Zama 14 B2
Zambezi, R. 4 D3, 6 D3,
   10 C2, 33 B4, 48 B-C3,
   54 C1, 56 D4, 57 D3
Zambia 1 D3, 55 B4,
   67 D3
Zamfara 36 C3, 43 B2,
   44 C1
Zande 50 D3
Zanj 28 C4, 42 B3
Zanjbar 42 B3
Zanzibar 26 D4, 33 B3,
   38 D4, 45 D2, 46 B4,
   47 B3, 49 E3, 50 D4,
   59 E3, 60 E3, 61 D4,
   63 D3, 64 D3, 65 D3,
   66 D4, 67 D3
Zarco, Gonçalves 38 B2
Zaria 35 C1, 36 C3,
   43 B2
Zaveces 15 C1
Zawila 29 B2, 30 C2,
   31 B2, 36 D2,
   37 C3
Zazo 19 B2
Zeekoe, R. 51 C2
Zembere 45 C3
Zenata 29 A2
Zimbabwe 48 C3
Zirids 30 B1
Zomba 67 D3
Zoutspanberg 52 D-E1
Zulu, Zululand 50 D5,
   52 E2, 53 C1, 60 E4,
   61 C-D5